———— *Taming Wild* ————

Taming Wild

The Compelling Origins
OF FREEDOM BASED TRAINING
and the Promise It Holds
FOR HORSES WITH HUMANS

ELSA SINCLAIR

Trafalgar Square
North Pomfret, Vermont

First published in 2025 by
Trafalgar Square Books
The Stable Book Group, Brooklyn, New York

Copyright © 2025 *Elsa Sinclair*

All rights reserved. No part of this book may be reproduced, by any means, without written permission of the publisher, except by a reviewer quoting brief excerpts for a review in a magazine, newspaper, or website.

Disclaimer of Liability
The author and publisher shall have neither liability nor responsibility to any person or entity with respect to any loss or damage caused or alleged to be caused directly or indirectly by the information contained in this book. While the book is as accurate as the author can make it, there may be errors, omissions, and inaccuracies.

Trafalgar Square Books encourages the use of approved safety helmets in all equestrian sports and activities.

Trafalgar Square Books certifies that the content in this book was generated by a human expert on the subject, and the content was edited, fact-checked, and proofread by human publishing specialists with a lifetime of equestrian knowledge. TSB does not publish books generated by artificial intelligence (AI).

Library of Congress Cataloging-in-Publication Data
Names: Sinclair, Elsa (Horse trainer), author.
Title: Taming wild : the compelling origins of freedom based training and the promise it holds for horses with humans / Elsa Sinclair.
Description: North Pomfret, Vermont : Trafalgar Square Books, 2024. | Includes index.
Identifiers: LCCN 2024028336 (print) | LCCN 2024028337 (ebook) | ISBN 9781646012596 (paperback) | ISBN 9781646012602 (epub)
Subjects: LCSH: Horses--Training.
Classification: LCC SF287 .S53 2024 (print) | LCC SF287 (ebook) | DDC 636.1/0835--dc23/eng/20240725
LC record available at https://lccn.loc.gov/2024028336
LC ebook record available at https://lccn.loc.gov/2024028337

Freedom Based Training® and Franklin Method® are registered and trademarked names. This notice serves to acknowledge this applies to all references used throughout this text.

Photos by *Kevin Smith*, *John Sinclair*, *Cameron Sinclair*, *Robert Lally*, *Arista Gates*, and *Mason Morfit* (Dedication)

Book design by *Katarzyna Misiukanis–Celińska (https://misiukanis-artstudio.com)*
Cover design by *RM Didier*
Index by *Andrea M. Jones (www.jonesliteraryservice.com)*
Typefaces: *Miller Text, Playfair Display* and *Domus*

Printed in China
10 9 8 7 6 5 4 3 2 1

this book
is dedicated
TO MY MOTHER

*A woman who taught me that two opposing things could be true simultaneously.
A woman who loved fiercely in the ways she thought best,
embracing chaos and peace within the same breath.*

*I refuse to be the child she raised, as I cannot love the extremes as she did.
However, admit I must, there is an untamed part of me that will forever be like my mother.
Loving fiercely in the ways I think best.*

*It is possible to both hate and love, both struggle and thrive,
be lost and found all wrapped up in one.*

*Here is to being unforgivably true to one's self,
while never giving up on becoming better than we were.*

Acknowledgments IX

The Beech 1

Part One: What Do I Do, When I Don't Know What to Do? 7
— *The Cost of Freedom*   9
— *An Undefinable Longing*   12
— *Searching*   16
— *A Glimpse of the Unknown*   19
— *Life-Changing Questions*   23
— *Thoughts Become Actions*   25

Part Two: Gathering Inspiration from Experience 29
— *Ransom*   31
— *Practical Learning Nightmares*   37
— *The Art of Paying Attention*   40
— *High Ideals*   47
— *Driven to Succeed*   52
— *Understanding Concern, Curiosity, and Comfort*   57
— *The Gift of Refocusing Pressure*   62
— *Feel and Timing*   71
— *Feeling Safe Enough*   81
— *A Horse's Hierarchy of Needs*   85
— *The Forest Holds Understanding*   92
— *Leadership Options*   98
— *Insistence*   103
— *Hugs Before Riding*   106
— *Bounces, Backups, and Bends Before Riding*   108
— *The Pre-Ride Pattern*   114

Part Three: Feelings Become More Important Than Actions 125
— *Emotions Within Actions*   127
— *Contrasts in Training*   135
— *Maybe It Isn't About Riding?*   142
— *Playing In Puddles*   146
— *Don't Rush the Process!*   148
— *Moving Home*   157
— *Too Slow!*   161
— *Thank Goodness for Storms*   166

The Beach 173

Appendix: Freedom Based Training—Points to Ponder 182
Index 187

ACKNOWLEDGMENTS

As a small child, if you had asked me what I wanted to be when I grew up, I would have told you I was going to train horses and write books. My grandfather would show me show jumpers and eventers and ask me if those were the things I was going to train horses to do when I grew up. And then he would seem baffled when I replied: "Oh no, nothing like that!"

If I was not THAT, then what was I?

As time passed, I met people who also wanted something different. I found horses who endlessly inspired me, and I realized I wasn't alone after all.

You know who you are, and if you are reading this, *we did it*. I couldn't have done it without you.

For all of you who believed in me when I didn't believe in myself, thank you. For all of you who held my vision for me in my moments of darkness, thank you. For all of you who questioned, thank you for feeding the fire inside me that longs always to learn more.

A special thank you to the photographers whose images appear in these pages: *Kevin Smith, John Sinclair, Cameron Sinclair, Robert Lally, Arista Gates, Mason Morfit*

Taming Wild
ELSA SINCLAIR

The Beech

/ 2 /

↓ The beech tree has watched over me through a million moments and twice as many emotions.

looking up at the crinkling leaves OF THE BEECH TREE PLANTED *in the paddock, it occurred to me* WE ARE ON THIS JOURNEY *together*

Thirty-five years before, we had both moved from the East Coast of the United States to the West Coast—Connecticut to Washington State. I was ten, and the beech tree was a sapling dug out of the forest, added last to the back of the moving van full of family possessions. Neither of us knew where we were going, but we were both young and resilient.

There'd actually been *three* saplings that moved with us, but only one had survived and grown tall in the northwest newness of rain and temperate gray skies. One out of three was adaptable enough to adjust—or maybe two out of four, if I counted myself in their number.

This tree has now watched over me for over thirty years. Watched horses come and go from this paddock as they taught me all the things I needed to know. Watched me cry, watched me laugh...watched me sometimes struggle against the horses as if they were adversaries instead of allies.

I wanted to thrive here; I *fought* to thrive here, as if fighting hard enough would keep me alive, like the one remaining beech tree. I wasn't rooted in life the way the tree was though. I thought I needed to fight for attention, fight for respect, fight for my place in the world. That was what I had been taught; how would I have known differently? I was a human, not a tree, after all.

It took me many years and the cooperation of a great many teachers (horses and humans alike) before I found a different way to thrive. Once I found it,

Myrnah

helped me see that training is natural, and force is optional.

of the wild, and a crazy idea that we could film a fairytale of a movie together—a story that might make people believe in magic for a moment. Myrnah helped me believe in it, beyond what I had thought was possible. Not the magic of spells and wishes, but a real deep and logical power that is in all of us.

Myrnah helped me see that *training* is natural, and force is optional.

Not the magic

of spells and wishes, but a real deep and logical power that is in all of us.

it took time and practice and an embarrassing amount of self-doubt before I could believe it was real. And even once I realized it was real, I thought perhaps it might be something I only could do in secret. My horses and I explored this new peaceful way of being together, under the beech tree, wrapped in the soft contemplative clouds of our home. But then out in the "real world," I put on my "game face" and fought the good fight of domination: humans over horses, shaping animals to our will, and cleverly describing dominion in a million creative words to soften the shackles of what we've long thought we *had* to do.

Myrnah changed this path for me; therefore, I am eternally grateful to the four-year-old Mustang mare, fresh out

Taming Wild
ELSA SINCLAIR

PART ONE

What Do I Do, When I Don't Know What to Do?

PART ONE

*What Do I Do,
When I Don't Know
What to Do?*

The Cost of Freedom

I was twelve years old and freedom was the ability to escape life on the back of my gritty Appaloosa mare, Demi.

Demi was my passport into the forest, away from people and the pressures of being what everyone else wanted me to be. That passport came at a price, and I had to fight for every moment. *Literally*, fight. Fight hard to stay on the horse, get thrown to the ground, get up bloody, and fight again for the freedom I so desperately wanted.

I wanted the peace of the forest. I wanted a friend in my horse, I wanted the two of us to run faster and jump higher than I could on my own two feet. I wanted the peace and harmony I had, at times, tasted with horses. But the only way I knew how to get close to what I wanted was to fight first so that peace was possible after each battle.

Demi was a fighter. She had gone into professional training at the age of three, like most horses, but refused to submit, ultimately bucking her trainer off so repeatedly that she was turned back out in the pasture and left untrained for the next five years.

At twelve years old I was the last child of my age group still riding a pony, and my mother decided it was time to find me a horse so I could continue my riding education with my peers. Why Demi seemed like a good choice for me, I will never know.

Our time together oscillated between moments of the deepest friendship and long bitter battles that left me scarred and more determined than ever to "win." I was bucked off at least weekly for over a year, and each time, my mother would say something to the tune of, "Good buckers make good jumpers," or "That horse is going to be amazing." Sometimes my mother was there to boost me back up on the irritated, barely containable mare, and other times I had a long walk home from whatever desolate place Demi had unceremoniously dumped me. I always climbed on again. I was well trained: *You never let them beat you—you get straight back on.*

I was taught my job was to *control the horse for everyone's safety.* When horses got "out of control," people got hurt. My mother let me learn this lesson the hard way, from my own mistakes and bruises, repeatedly. In hindsight, it was cleaner than learning the "easy" way with someone instructing me how better to apply the pressure of leg, rein, and whip.

I was enrolled in dressage lessons, to better learn how to control the horse, *so no one got hurt,* or at least, hurt less often. Fancy instructors flew out on a tiny plane for a day of instruction on the small island I lived on, and a neighbor kindly let the local horse community gather at her arena to study. It was the one day of the week I practiced in a proper area instead of in circles around slippery pastures.

The problem was getting there. The arena was within riding distance and no farther away from home than our regular trail rides; however, it only took a couple of experiences for Demi to decide she didn't want to go to dressage lessons.

Dressage lessons were part of the price we had to pay for our freedom on the trails, though. Neither of us had the autonomy to walk away from our relationship, or the requirements placed on us by those who held power over us. So we fought the good fight to get the job done and earn us the occasional escape into the forest.

Only once did I miss a dressage lesson.

Demi got partway down the dirt road between home and the arena and stopped. Turning in circles and flicking the dressage whip did no more than stimulate kicking and bucking, which I now, due to much practice, knew how to sit. The clock was ticking...I was going to be late...I was going to be in so much trouble if I wasted my parents' money and the instructor's time.

With tears streaming down my face and teeth gritted, I turned the whip up in my hand. Pointed to the sky with the full force of my arm behind it, I cracked it down on my horse: *left side, right side, left side, right side.* The bucking and the kicking temporarily stopped in the face of my brutality, but Demi refused to be intimidated into forward momentum. Each time the whip cracked down she grunted and involuntarily flinched an inch or two forward, with me hoping each inch gained was the last bit of resistance we would have to fight through.

I don't know how long I fought her. It felt like hours of senseless battle before I turned, defeated, riding in the only direction Demi would willingly travel. When we came to a neighbor's house, I stopped and borrowed their phone to call the organizer for the day's lesson, and through broken sobs, I admitted I would not be able to make it in time. I couldn't get my horse past the line she had drawn in the gravel halfway down our road. Or at least I couldn't do it fast enough to make the lesson time deadline.

What followed was one of the most horrible weeks of my life. I didn't have the knowledge to fix the problem I was facing, but I was told by my mother I must fix it. So every day, Demi and

> *I was taught my job was*
>
> *to control the horse for everyone's safety. When horses got "out of control," people got hurt. My mother let me learn this lesson the hard way, from my own mistakes and bruises.*

I revisited her line in the gravel road that she would not cross. Each day we fought a brutal uneducated fight of tears and aggression that got us no farther than a few strides more down the road, hard won. It was a fight neither of us would have chosen, but we were in a situation we didn't know how to excuse ourselves from.

By the end of the week and the next scheduled dressage lesson, I had succeeded and could again ride the half hour to the schooling arena. It was a hollow victory that pleased my teacher, my mother, and my peers. They didn't know the cost, and I never told them.

Through fulfilling my obligations of riding education and dressage lessons, I earned my passport to freedom, back to the woods and the peace of nature with my beloved mare. But it was a complicated love between us.

— An Undefinable Longing

That is not what I mean, I want something different.

The words in my head were emphatic and frustrated. The voice I sent down the phone line was softer, timid, and questioning. I knew better than to be too loud or too demanding. If I wanted my father to talk to me, I must be reasonable, and gentle, and show him I respected his words beyond mine.

I *was* frustrated though. I wanted peace and harmony in my life with horses, and everywhere I turned, I was told that was only won through necessary fights.

My father—a well-educated man, but not a horse person—was doing his best to hear me out. Horses were something my mother and I did together, and my father was a bystander, perhaps a bit bewildered by our obsession. I only saw him on holidays and a few weeks every summer, but he did his best to be there for me over the phone, providing an outside perspective when I asked for it.

He had brought up the idea of *positive reinforcement* as a solution to my frustration with horse training. It wasn't a bad idea, but it wasn't what I was looking for, and he wasn't hearing me. I read books endlessly, I studied with every horse trainer I thought might know something more than me. I was familiar with the black-and-white camps of *positive reinforcement* versus *negative reinforcement*. I wanted something different!

I could define *positive reinforcement* as *adding something good* to horses' lives when they offered the correct behaviors. I could define *negative reinforcement* as *releasing the pressure* of leg, rein, or whip when they offered the correct behaviors. The problem was that I couldn't

↓ The love between Demi and me was complicated with twists and turns of events that shaped us both.

↓ Demi allowed me to run faster and jump higher than my own feet could carry me.

Ironically,

I was internally bracing myself to fight for what I wanted, when what I wanted was to stop fighting.

↓ Horse shows were not our cup of tea, but we wouldn't back down from a challenge either.

clearly define what I was looking for that was different than those options. I just knew what I wanted wasn't being offered by the books I'd read or the trainers I'd seen. I wanted a teacher to appear with the magic solution that allowed me to spend time with horses without "forcing them" to do things they didn't want to do. I didn't want to "force them" through a carefully regulated distribution of food, and I didn't want to "force them" through intimidation. I knew what I *didn't* want, but I also didn't know anyone who believed it was possible to train horses any other way.

Ironically, I was internally bracing myself to fight for what I wanted, when what I wanted was to stop fighting.

/ PART I / What Do I Do, When I Don't Know What to Do?

Searching

At seventeen I drove to every clinic I could reach that allowed me to study Linda Tellington-Jones's Tellington TTouch and Tellington Equine Awareness Method as it felt like the first step I had found in the direction of something different, working *with* horses more than *against* them. This opened new worlds for me, as I springboarded from her work to further studying the Alexander Technique and the Feldenkrais Method, where the way I carried my body would innately affect my horses in positive ways beyond what I had imagined possible. At the time, these areas of study felt like groundbreaking ways to access a horse's desire to work cooperatively with others.

I was young and impatient and excited about every new nugget of an idea presented. I remember one Tellington-Jones clinic where she had participants riding around an arena with neck ropes only—without halters or bridles on the horses' heads. The feeling! I wanted more of it!

I promptly went home after the clinic and got on my beautiful Arabian mare Shameeka with only a saddle and a neck rope. She was perfect—we had left turns and right turns and stops, so I headed out on the trail into the peace of the forest with a new degree of freedom I had never experienced before. It was heaven…until about forty-five minutes out, when Shameeka decided she had enough and turned and galloped all the way home.

I clearly had more to learn before I could earn the next evolution of freedom, which I had just tasted. How could I know a horse was ready to coexist more freely with me without putting us in a situation where one or both of us could be harmed? Grasping for the control I thought I needed, I leaned into the study of Centered Riding®, a way of learning and applying classical principles of riding through body awareness and imagery. Perhaps if I could just sit well enough on a horse, breathe well enough,

How could I know

a horse was ready to coexist more freely with me without putting us in a situation where one or both of us could be harmed?

be balanced enough, then my horse and I could be both free and safe together?

From those first attempts at age of seventeen to a decade later, I would like to say I was gathering the skills I would need later in life, but at the time it felt like an endless struggle to figure out who I was and what I wanted.

I raced endurance horses for a while. I taught children to ride ponies. I studied French classical dressage, eventing, jumping, and Parelli® Natural Horsemanship. I learned to play polocrosse and took endless forays down trails and into the forest to feel the freedom all this was supposed to be supporting.

I took time away from horses to be a nanny and tried to make it in the big city with the new career goal of becoming a dancer. I gave that up to hitchhike around Costa Rica and sleep on beaches with friends. I fell in love, had a child, and moved overseas. I was still searching for peace, harmony, and freedom, just in different places.

At the age of thirty, it all changed.

My marriage ended, and with my six-year-old daughter, I moved back to the island where I'd grown up to live next-door to my mother and stepfather's home.

My mother was still managing a herd of twenty horses with almost as many children of all ages coming and going every day to ride them. It made sense for me to help, and before long I was remembering all the joys and frustrations, and the deep longing being with horses brought up in me.

I still wanted more...but I didn't even know what *more* looked like.

↓ Ransom let me feel like I was good at something, but he was better at everything than I was.

A Glimpse of the Unknown

Life happened. I found myself needing to make money with a pressure I had never felt before. That need led to long days, traveling off-island and into the city to teach every form of horsemanship I knew. There was no shortage of work if I was willing to travel and adapt and show clients of all types the skills they needed to achieve their goals with their horses. I had decades of experience to pull from, and everywhere I went, I could spread better understanding of horses and a little more joy for those working with them—everyone except maybe myself.

I pulled into each farm to teach a few lessons—from loading horses into trailers, to achieving better equitation in the saddle; from children learning to halter a new pony, to adults learning to be brave again after years away from these big animals. And as I got back in my truck to drive on to the next farm or arena, I would cry my eyes out—not the polite tears you cry when someone is watching, but the ugly ones that shed anger, pain, and frustration under the guise of sadness. Sometimes the cause was the cold, exhaustion, or the knowledge that my feet were wet and probably wouldn't be dry for another ten hours because I had forgotten to pack extra socks. Sometimes it was the toll it took on me to pressure a horse into a trailer or away from a herd mate. Most often it was the light I saw dim in other people's eyes as I showed them the way to win a fight with their horses to earn the "freedom" they thought they wanted. Forty to sixty minutes later, I would pull into the next farm and find my composure again, knowing it was time to show up, do the work, and be grateful for having it.

I liked being good at something. I liked earning enough money to feed my family. I was kind, logical, and gentle, with horses and humans, to the extent I knew how to be. I wanted to save them all the pain I had gone through when I had no one to show me how to win a fight better.

I was doing good in the world. I was training horses and their humans to think cooperatively with as few conflicts as possible to get there. I was also torn to pieces by what I didn't know, wanted to know, and didn't know how to learn.

Then, I met an unusual woman who changed everything for me.

Kathleen was a high-powered businesswoman who had grown up with horses, left them behind for her career, and was now looking for a way to reconnect. The first day I met her she brought an album of photographs, pictures she had taken of horses over the recent years. She said she was looking for a trainer to help her with something different, and the best way to explain that difference was to have me look at the photographs.

We opened the album on top of a wooden barrel in the aisle of the barn I was teaching at that day, and I put on the best thoughtful expression I had in hopes of winning her approval and the job as we looked through the pages. As I considered the photographs, I had a glimmer of a feeling, but it wasn't a feeling I could put into words if she had asked me to explain what it was I thought she wanted. That was okay though, as she was showing me the pictures because she couldn't put the feeling into words either.

Did I think I could help her? Yes. Did I have any clear idea how? No.

Here was a kindred spirit, though, someone who could say she wanted *more* from her relationship with horses, but like me, couldn't quite put her finger on what that *more* looked like. I was not going to pass up the opportunity to be part of discovering what that looked like for her. Besides, I really needed the money, and every client who wanted to trade money for my time was someone I could help, and someone I would *find a way to help*, whatever that took.

Like me, Kathleen was a morning person, happy to meet at five in the morning, before anyone else was ready. We would borrow a horse from one of my other clients, and in the quiet of a barn not yet awake, we would "play." I watched and offered an outside perspective and insight into patterns that evolved between Kathleen and the horse. The goal, it seemed, was to have both horse and human enjoy their time together, equally. It wasn't about making the horse do a particular thing, it wasn't about food rewards or scratching rewards, or any kind of rewards at all. It was simply about being together with a curiosity about what might happen next. Over time, these once-a-week "play sessions" seemed to develop both horse and human into better versions of themselves.

↓ Zohari set the bar higher for me than any horse I had known before him. What I didn't know, I had to learn.

↓ Saavedra was my first wild horse, a Mustang who knew her own mind.

Not because that was the aim, but simply because that was the natural evolution of the situation.

You might think being part of something like this was exactly what I was looking for—a situation where horse and human were both developing and seeming to improve without the fight or manipulation I had been taught was necessary to be with horses safely. However, once I had tasted a little of it, I wanted more, and the only way I knew how to get more at that time was to push harder.

Looking back, I am grateful to Kathleen for stubbornly ignoring me when I suggested she be more manipulative or pointed with her actions. I would push her to do something different with her body that I felt might have a better outcome or response from the horse, and Kathleen would push back and say something like, "I just want to see what happens if I do this other thing that I am curious about first."

Kathleen was paying me to be an observer of her experimental process, and she welcomed my thoughts on developing patterns, but she was not interested in my directions. She made her own decisions and discovered for herself the outcome with the horse for each decision she made.

This was new and frustrating territory for me as a teacher.

Life-Changing Questions

One day Kathleen asked me a series of questions that quietly turned my life upside down.

"Do you think horses really enjoy being ridden?"

I said, "Yes, I think they do."

So then she asked, "What if they hadn't been trained to it from birth? What if they had an independent sense of who they are and knew they had a choice about being ridden?"

I thought for a moment and replied, "People bring Mustangs in from the range all the time, and even at older ages, train them to be great riding companions."

Then Kathleen asked, "Do you really think the horses know they have a choice?"

At that moment, all of a sudden, I had no answer.

If I didn't know the answer to this question, did anyone else? I spent the next few weeks researching and asking everyone I knew if there was any trainer who had trained a horse to be ridden without food rewards or the pressure of entrapment between human and halter or human and fence.

Caroline Resnick, founder of The Resnick Method Liberty Horsemanship, was perhaps the closest I could find who had attempted to broach the idea in her book *Naked Liberty*. Years before, I had spent some time practicing the beginnings of her method, but I had ultimately left it, thinking it was just something else shiny that had caught my attention. Revisiting her training ideas with Kathleen's queries in mind, I found it centered around food in a way that seemed would cloud the question of choice. Horses will do quite a lot for access to food, even when they are not "hungry" in an essential way. As humans, we can easily exploit this by systematically offering but then withholding food ("treats") until we get behaviors we want. We can dress up the theory in different ways and lean so hard into the positive aspects that the negative aspects are forgotten, but it is still the horse's "fear of lack" in some way that builds new behaviors. And it was *this* that had always felt like an uncomfortable amount of power over the horse to me.

So I wondered: How could I set up an experiment to answer Kathleen's questions?

I would need to work exclusively with one horse, and I felt that one horse would have to be a wild horse that had lived its formative years free to make its own decisions without human interference. Before the horse could answer questions about *freedom of choice*, I needed to be sure the horse was comfortable *being free* to begin with.

This horse would need to have horse friends so that humans were a possible added benefit to life, but not a necessary part.

The horse would need to have food available all the time, preferably free-choice as part of the environment and not delivered by humans in any obvious way that might indirectly manipulate the horse's decisions.

The horse would need space—as much space as possible so it could walk away from a human it was not interested in interacting with.

I thought that if this experiement had never been done before (in a way that was recorded) then someone should do it!

I spent weeks thinking about the project and telling every horse person who would listen about it. I didn't have time for such an experiment. I had a daughter to raise and a job to maintain. My life was full.

But over time it became clear that no one else I talked to was as interested in this idea as I was, so I began to think perhaps it could be my "retirement project." At sixty-five, perhaps, I would have saved up enough money to take the time it would take to engage with a horse in the way I imagined. Until then, I could dream about it. What would I need to know to run an experiment like that? What would a wild horse need from me before it would *want* to carry me on its back?

Thoughts Become Actions

Within a few months, I had talked about my "retirement project" so frequently to so many people it had taken on a life of its own. Thirty-five years was a long time to plan for a project this interesting, and I am not a patient person. I want what I want, and I want it now. All my talk of future goals and plans caught the attention of John, a friend and client, and he asked, "Why not do it now?"

I had what felt like a million good reasons to wait, but the most pressing was that I didn't have the money or the time to devote to the project. I had good work and a lot of it, but it took all my time to make the money I needed to keep my family afloat.

I had excuses and John had solutions.

"What if you adopted two Mustangs, one for your project and one to train for me?" he proposed. "Would the income from training the second Mustang help you have enough money to free up your time?"

His offer was tempting. Could I make it work?

"I don't have a big enough truck to haul two Mustangs home from Oregon or Nevada," I said, still doubtful.

But John had a big truck and trailer, and he wanted to go with me to pick out the horses.

"Let me think about it..." I remained hesitant. Pausing before accepting such an offer was important. I wanted to be a responsible parent for my daughter. I wanted to plan my future in a logical and sensible way.

The hook had been set though. I could see how, just maybe, I could have my cake and eat it too. If I worked hard enough on weekends, and John paid me to train a second Mustang for him, perhaps I could devote five days a week to my experiment and see where it took me. I wanted my vision of peace, harmony, and voluntary cooperation with horses, and I believed the experiment might prove it was a valid option. I was so tempted by this vision that I was willing to push myself as hard as I needed to for the logistics to work out.

I gave myself six months to get my ducks in a row. I would study, I would practice, I would make all the right phone calls to all the right people, and by the time Mustangs were being rounded up from the range in the summer of 2011, I would be ready.

With a handshake, John and I had a deal and a plan.

– END OF PART ONE –

*What Do I Do,
When I Don't Know
What to Do?*

Taming Wild
ELSA SINCLAIR

PART TWO

Gathering Inspiration from Experience

PART TWO

*Gathering Inspiration
from Experience*

Ransom

On January 1, 2011, I started a blog to help map out and process my ideas. I thought that if I committed to posting every week, perhaps by summer I would have a clearer idea of how my experiment might have a successful outcome.

I started by writing about the horses I had trained in the past. What had I learned from each one of them? How could I take those experiences and use them to shape a new program? I was imagining a training progression where the horse was never trapped between me and a fence, never experienced the feel of a rope, the threat of a flag, the withholding of food, or the separation from a herd. I knew I was somewhat limited in my ability to follow these ideals. The wild horse I was going to work with was going to need to come to my home, which meant there would be some entrapment before freedom began anew. Through the adoption process, the government required an enclosure of six-foot-tall panels. Even making this space as big as I could afford to fence, it wasn't possible to have an entire herd of horses in there. A single friend would have to suffice until it felt safe enough to move the Mustangs into more open space with modest fencing.

As I wrote my blog each week, I seemed to come up with more questions than answers, and six months started to feel like not enough time.

I needed a *core theory*—a central concept I could lean on and take action around, until the many questions found their answers. I was going to start this experiment before I was ready, but what was my core idea that would make me just ready enough?

The answer to that question came from a Thoroughbred off the racetrack that I had been given as a re-start project. Ransom, or "High Tech Exec" if you want to laugh at his racing name, was the most socially adept horse I have ever met. I don't know how he learned his skills; all I can conclude is that he must have had a very good mother.

Ransom was turned out with our herd of twenty horses, and I never saw him bite, kick, or threaten another. Yet within about ten days, he seemed to hold a remarkable degree of leadership in the group. Anything Ransom wanted to do, the other horses seemed to want to do too.

I wondered, if he didn't bite, kick, or threaten to earn that social status, what did he do?

I observed with interest as he alternated action and passivity with a timing that shaped everyone's feelings associated with him. When the herd was agitated, he just kept moving, kept out of trouble, and didn't settle until everyone else had settled first. Then, he would pick one friend, just one horse that got all his attention. Ransom would move around that one horse until the horse was comfortable with where Ransom was in relation to him, and then Ransom would stop and be like the friend horse, passively.

If the herd got unsettled again for any reason, Ransom would stay active and out of trouble. Only after the herd was quiet again would he go back to the friend he had chosen, and he would continue to pay attention to this horse through alternating action and passivity until the horse appeared to become quite fond of him. Then Ransom would move on to the next friend and repeat the pattern. It took Ransom about ten days to work through each horse in the herd of twenty.

I had never seen equine social skills quite like his, and it was remarkable enough for me to take note. The pattern of using *action* alternating with *passivity in harmony* (being with horses in partnership while being *non-distracting* to allow them to feel all their own feelings) was going to be my *core theory* for my experiment.

If I acted like Ransom around a wild Mustang, would the Mustang accept me into its herd in the same way? Could I be as skilled as Ransom, or skilled enough to get similar results?

Ransom was the horse that showed me the core theory for Freedom Based Training.

/ PART II / *Gathering Inspiration from Experience*

↓ Saavedra was comfortable with the black-and-white clarity of dominance-based training, and wanted no part of my early uneducated attempts at Freedom Based Training.

Practical Learning Nightmares

In the summer, our herd of twenty ran together, but in the wet winter months, they were divided up into more manageable groups and locations. During my early days of prep time, I had four mares living in a pasture next to my house. These were the horses I used for my first trials that tested ideas of freedom. I failed miserably.

Saavedra probably helped me the most out of all the mares. She was the first Mustang I'd ever adopted, seven years before. She was black as night with a white star and ankle, and had come from the Sheldon National Wildlife Refuge in Nevada. Saavedra had been my first tentative attempts with the possibility that less pressure might be more effective, although my ideas of "less pressure" at that time in my life were still far from the freedom I longed for. While I may have been exploring a "better" dominance-based training, it was still dominance-based training. In the six months preceding my planned experiment, as a horse that had once been wild, Saavedra helped me understand *what freedom was* and *what it wasn't* in the context of training. She did this with clear defiance of any agenda of mine that might be trying to masquerade as "freedom."

I had a problem. I wanted to learn everything I needed to know in a hurry. Every day I found myself spending time asking the horses ceaselessly if they would interact with me *in freedom*. But I couldn't take no for an answer. I was on a deadline! I would follow them around without pause, as if the pressure of my desire would somehow win them to my cause. The mares would humor me for brief moments but often avoided the intensity of my company instead. Who could blame them?

Saavedra responded best to clear and dominant expressions of my desires in patterns she was familiar with. She was well trained in a dominance-based way, so it didn't take much pressure anymore to ask her to

Saavedra met me on her terms; if someone needed to adapt, it was me, not her.

do tasks. However, if I didn't have a stick or rope in my hand, she wasn't particularly interested in "talking" to or interacting with me. This was endlessly frustrating for me, and at the time, I found myself returning to systems we knew when nothing else seemed to be working. This was an option I wouldn't have with the new Mustang in the project ahead.

I wasn't quite sure what I was going to do about that. I did find I could work around Saavedra in the ways that Ransom had shown me. I could find the moments where harmony was easy and match my body to hers. This told me the beginning of my core theory was solid... but what next? I wanted her *to want* my company. I wanted her to want to do things with me. I wanted to feel her connection to me. It seemed I wanted this relationship much more than she did. It seemed I just couldn't manage the active/passive language as well as Ransom could. I began to wonder if perhaps my experiment was a failure before it was even truly started.

Saavedra demonstrated to me with her behavior where her *comfort zone* was— she was comfortable being told what to do with a clear tool of reinforcement, such as a flag or a stick or a rope. I didn't have enough understanding to be able to shape a new pattern or a new comfort zone where tools were not needed to achieve this, but that was exactly my aim: I wanted to build a comfort zone for us that held within it freedom of choice and positive associations to me and doing things with me, without the

↓ Saavedra and Yahzi were gathered from the Sheldon National Wildlife Refuge in northwest Nevada.

need for the pressure tools provided. Every day I tried again: behave like Ransom, watch the patterns of the four mares, offer my connection to Saavedra without needing for her to give connection back to me.

What would it take for a horse to be as interested as I was in forming a relationship and doing things together?

Most days I would fail at making progress toward answering this question, and would end with the thought, *Perhaps tomorrow I will figure it out*. I was learning to face a fact: I wanted a lot from horses, all the time, and that didn't make me an easy partner to be around. Were the horses going to change, or was I?

/ PART II / *Gathering Inspiration from Experience*

The Art of Paying Attention

In the muddle of trying training actions "in freedom" around my horses, giving up, and trying again, my friend Margaret asked me what the plan was to record my upcoming experiment. I knew documenting the process was one of the primary reasons for the project, but I had been pointedly ignoring that detail. In my state of feeling deeply unsure of an actual path to success with a new Mustang in the way I imagined, I really didn't want to think about how much it might wound my pride to record and share a year's worth of failures.

Margaret suggested I plan to film the process—and not just "set a tripod" up in a corner of a paddock, but *really* film it, as if it was going to become a documentary. At the time, Margaret was working in that capacity, making films, and I knew she was very good at it. But I didn't have the money to pay her.

"What if nothing happens for the next year other than me sitting in a pasture with a horse?" I worried. "What if there is nothing interesting at all to document?"

Margaret had known me for a long time, and I had always admired her quiet way of saying just the right thing with a minimum of words.

"I'm pretty sure something will happen."

Margaret helped me find the right camera to buy and offered to come with me and John to the Oregon Bureau of Land Management (BLM) corrals to film the Mustangs just after roundup and prior to coming home with us. She then offered to visit me once a month through the entire year of the project to film whatever did or did not happen. She said I could pay her if I ever did turn the footage into a documentary.

Turns out, Margaret believed in me more than I believed in myself at that point in time.

↓ Margaret, out on the range, northwest Nevada.

/ PART II / *Gathering Inspiration from Experience*

So in August of 2011, John, Margaret, and I pulled into the parking area at the BLM corrals in Burns, Oregon, to choose two Mustangs. I was grateful for the good people who had offered to help me with my crazy idea. I had even managed to talk the government offices into supporting my experiment by waiving their usual holding requirements for Mustangs of several months in the official corrals. They were allowing me to watch the latest gather of wild horses as they were unloaded from trailers at the main facility, just hours after they had been rounded up by helicopter. I would choose a mare without a foal at her side, and a companion meant to be for John, the BLM would brand them and give them the first round of vaccinations and worming medicine, and load them onto our trailer. This fast track enabled me to have the Mustangs home within a couple of days and was a real gift for the purpose of the experiment. I wanted to be able to bounce all my ideas off a horse that was as wild and free as possible. I wanted this horse's honest opinion about *my* decisions while she still remembered what it was like to be free to make all *her own* decisions.

The irony of how much I wanted some intangible thing having to do with freedom, yet was starting the project by taking away the freedom of a wild creature was not lost on me. I understood I held the power as I searched with my binoculars

↓ Myrnah's ability to pay attention beyond the capacity of all the other horses was an attribute I would learn in time was a gift beyond measure.

↓ The loss of Myrnah's real freedom was felt deeply. We both could only guess at what life might be like beyond this point.

/ PART II / *Gathering Inspiration from Experience*

↓ Through all the trials of gathering, sorting, and traveling, Myrnah's grace shone beyond her confines.

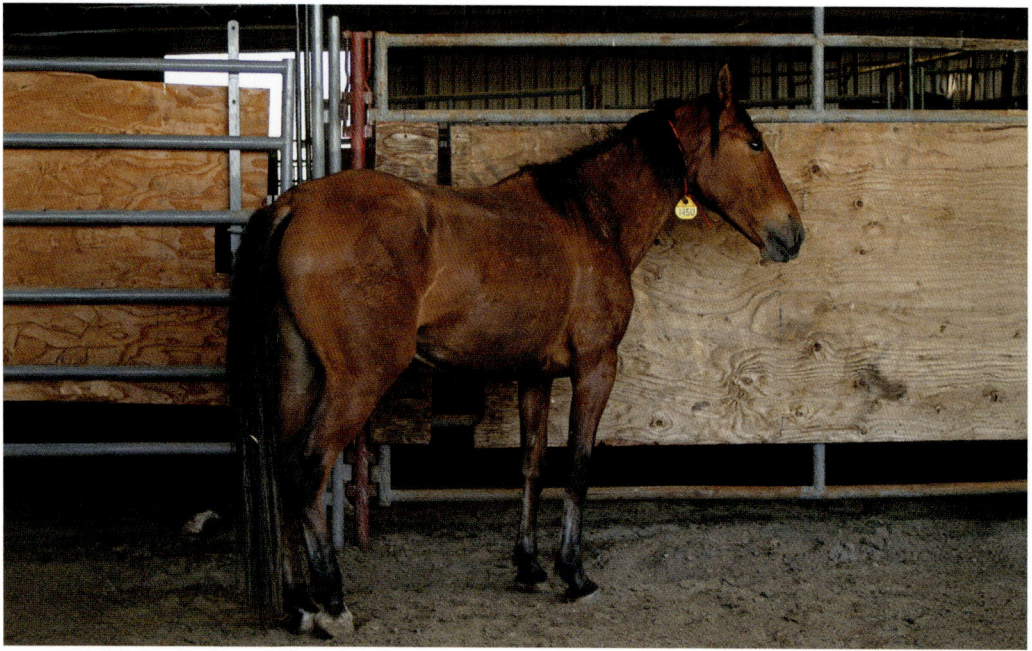

through the undulating bodies of horses as they pushed around and past each other in endless circles, trying to adapt to the small new spaces. They crashed hard into metal panels, testing their horse strength against human walls, but they didn't know what it was they were running away from or what was pushing them toward panic.

Adapt they did though, with chaos sorting itself into synchronicity. Fight and flight could only go on without success for so long before the horses started working together again. Bodies found their place in space in harmony with all the other bodies and eyes and ears as they gathered new information from the overwhelming world around them. And this information-gathering as a group could only go on for so long

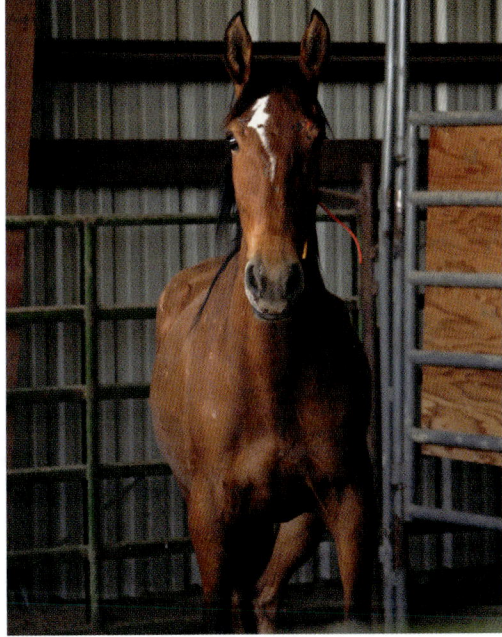

Myrnah's character was as striking as her lightning blaze.

before the horses needed to rest in turns, ears dropping out to the sides and eyelids getting heavy. A strange sound or sight would bring them all back to high alert, sometimes all the way back to fight or flight...but, again, it was only a matter of time before they settled back into synchronicity and then, a few at a time, into the necessary rest of deep exhaustion.

This group of horses was showing me their characters, their emotional strengths and weaknesses, their tendencies to be more defensive or more cooperative, but I didn't yet know how to read all that. I was grasping for the right body conformation and trying to find the horse that was built best for riding on. I was looking at the straightness of the legs and the symmetry of the left- and right-side muscling. At that time, those were the only parameters I knew how to measure and compare.

It wasn't until John and Margaret and I were in the hotel that night, going over the footage Margaret had filmed at the corrals, that I saw Myrnah. She didn't fit any of the physical parameters I was looking for, but she ticked all the emotional boxes I didn't yet know how to assess. The only way I could describe it at the time was, *she looked at the camera when no one else did.*

Myrnah's ability to pay attention beyond the capacity of all the other horses was an attribute I would learn in time was a gift beyond measure. At least, it was if I wanted a partner who could think for herself.

↓ Cleo and Myrnah in their new home. What would they teach me?

High Ideals

We drove all night to get the two new Mustangs home—one chosen by me on a "feeling" criteria I could not yet fully explain, and one chosen by John for his own riding goals.

I could feel the pressure building.

Margaret had given her time and expertise filming. John had supported me with the faith and the means to start the project. My family had helped me build the high-fenced corrals we needed, and my students and friends had cheered me on every step of the way. Now it was my turn to step up and make the experiment successful.

I couldn't proceed the way I would normally in training a horse because I had taken away all my usual training tools. I had to find a *new way*...but I still didn't know what that new way was.

Ransom had given me a key—I knew being a leader had something to do with the actions I took around the horses, alternating with the quiet moments that we enjoyed together. Beyond that key, though, I only had my history of pressure-based training to draw on. How could I use that but more gently? Gently enough that two wild horses, right off the range, would want to stay with me more than they would want to get away from me?

Ransom had also shown me that *timing* was important; *when* I did things mattered.

Saavedra, when I worked with her in her early days and then later in the group of four mares, as I prepared for my project, had given me the idea of *feel*—a starting place for *what* I would do.

When I had adopted Saavedra, years before, the BLM handlers had offered to put a halter on her with a dragline when she was in the chutes, before she was funneled into my trailer. The halter and dragline were

↓ Saavedra had let me play with lowering the pressure of training; now Myrnah and Cleo were going to show me how go deeper. What if the fences held no threat of pressure? What if we worked together instead of as adversaries?

supposed to help me get her halter trained once she was home. While the offer was well-intentioned, I was appalled at the idea.

Even then, *I wanted freedom, not coercion!* This contradiction of ideas was a throughline of frustration again and again in my life. There I was, taking a wild-and-free four-year-old off the range and bringing her into captivity where I would ask her to do things I wanted her to do, while paying lip service to "freedom." I didn't know how to get the freedom I wanted to feel with her, but I knew forcing a halter and drag line on my new Mustang was not where I wanted to start.

That first foray into training Mustangs brought home four-year-old Saavedra and a yearling filly for one of my students. It was an exciting event on San Juan Island, drawing friends and neighbors to the farm, where they set up folding chairs outside small temporary pens to watch my student and me begin the gentling process. At that time, too, I had high ideals for a training method with less pressure, and my goal was to use eye contact as a more subtle source of pressure instead of the usual ropes or flags to intimidate the Mustangs into submission. I hoped that eye contact, or the removal of it, would influence the horses into changing a behavior or doing something cooperative.

Ideals gave way to reality, however, and the reality at that time was that our training pens were

↓ Taking off a Mustang's identification tag is a celebrated moment with a new wild one. Sometimes, it feels like a victory in the battle against time and instinct; other times we get it more right, and it feels like a victory because we are returning some small semblance of freedom.

very small—much too small for the comfort of newly captured mustangs. When my student and I stepped inside their pens to join the horses, they would run around and around, trying to escape. It turned out that the combination of eye contact and physical proximity was a great deal more pressure than I had thought it would be.

We pushed on, even though the pressure was higher than I had wanted. Higher pressure was familiar territory, and I knew how to win this "fight" with the horse in order to eventually earn the freedom we both wanted. In time Saavedra and the yearling, who we called Yahzi, learned that looking at us with curiosity instead of trying to run away was a better way to relieve the pressure of our eye contact and close proximity. This realization developed until they learned that continuing to look at us perpetuated continued release of pressure. Then, the two horses discovered that when you look at a human long enough, it eventually becomes irresistible to get a little closer to see what more you can begin to understand about this strange creature. This evolved into learning that humans sometimes had ropes that, like eye contact, were just another form of pressure that could also be eased with enough curiosity. Saavedra and Yahzi learned these ropes were the key to a kind of freedom, enabling them to move outside their small pens to be reunited with a herd of new friends in a big open space.

/ PART II / *Gathering Inspiration from Experience*

↓ First contact always feels better when it is reciprocal—both reaching out and meeting in the middle.

Gaining all that understanding only took a week for four-year-old Saavedra, and ten days for the yearling Yahzi. It wasn't training in freedom, it wasn't training without pressure, but it was the closest I had come to training with *less* pressure—and I wanted more.

Four years later, I was unloading two bay-colored, four-year-old Mustang mares on San Juan Island. I had chosen Myrnah for my project and John had chosen Cleo to be a potential future endurance racing partner. The plan was I would keep both mares together for a year at my home: first in the high-fenced corrals close to my house, and then, as soon as possible, integrated into the herd of twenty on the large expanse of pastures in the valley on my family's farm. Myrnah and I would be exploring our project of "freedom" together while I took Cleo's training on a more standard path in preparation for her life with John.

This time I endeavored to make the initial spaces bigger, so I could use eye contact for pressure without pushing the mares up against the fences or into a run. I wanted to use the same idea I had with Saavedra but with less urgency when it came to time and bigger distances between us. This time I would do it better!

What defines better? *An awareness of feel and timing adapted to the horse.*

Adapting "feel" to horses means choosing actions that do not irritate or scare them. But the more important thing that must be adapted to the horse is "timing"—starting an action before horses need to take action to defend themselves, ceasing the action at a moment they have more curiosity about life and relationships than they have fear, and then allowing them to rest and meditate on all that is right and good in their life. It is impossible to get the timing right all the time, but it is a game of averages. Can we get it more right than wrong?

↓ The first moments of gathering information about each other through the five senses feel precious beyond belief.

Only the horse can tell us if we are getting it *right enough*.

When we see increasing amounts of concern in the horse, it shows in signs of fight or flight, which means either our feel or our timing is off by a lot. When we see increasing amounts of curiosity, shown by synchrony and the use of the horse's senses (seeing, hearing, smelling, feeling, or tasting), we are doing something right.

When horses trust us enough to have moments of rest in our company, shown by a lack of sensory awareness (eyes no longer looking to see, ears no longer moving, nostrils no longer smelling, body no longer stretching into a feeling, investigative tasting turned to the routine of eating), they may even remember the things we did right today and trust us a little more tomorrow.

Trust isn't all or nothing; it is associated with good feelings that get remembered. How do we build associations like this? It might look like this from the horse's point of view: *The last time the human rested a hand on my shoulder, did it make me feel better or worse? If it made me feel better, I want them to repeat it again tomorrow. If it made me feel worse, I want to avoid or defend against it tomorrow. If it made me feel nothing and I slept through it, I probably won't remember it enough to have an educated opinion on it tomorrow.*

The rest moments are important, but horses don't gather more information while they are resting, they process the information they gathered *before* the resting began.

/ PART II / *Gathering Inspiration from Experience*

Driven to Succeed

In the first week with Myrnah, my tendency to be impatient and pushy might have done us a favor without me realizing at the time.

I was driven; I had given myself only one year for my project and I wanted it to succeed. That meant I needed to pour myself into it and grasp every opportunity I could to progress my new horse's training. My reasoning was that without tools or entrapments or rewards, Myrnah was going to have full control of this timeline because she would be able to simply walk away from me if I pushed her more than she wanted to be pushed. I assumed I wouldn't have many actual opportunities to progress the timeline on my end, and therefore I had to use *every one* that appeared—*if* I was to have any chance of success at all. Later this perspective would bite me, but that first week, it helped me grasp a basic concept of timing I didn't fully understand yet.

This concept was that *passivity must have a better association than action if you want to train in freedom.*

We are not talking about the black and white of "good" and "bad" here, but the spectrum shades of gray—"better" or "worse." How could I make one association "better" than another? Horses could only want more of something they feel they didn't get enough of. Using this in training was something I learned accidentally, and I am forever grateful for my mistakes that eventually led to understanding.

That first week, I grasped at every opportunity to *take action* around Myrnah: to approach her and move away from her before she moved away from me....to touch her and retreat before it was overwhelming to her...to stroke more of her body...to remove the rope and the number tag from the government corrals that was around her neck...to handle her legs and start picking up her feet. *So much action.*

↓ The action of picking up a hoof was no more or less difficult than the actions of approaching or touching or stroking or retreating—just different.

/ PART II / *Gathering Inspiration from Experience*

↖↖↓ Each new action presented a novelty of feeling that tickled the senses in a good way. Action and passivity, alternating at the correct times, was our recipe for success.

Because I took every opportunity Myrnah allowed me for *more action*, it became the predominant way we related to each other. For the most part, my "feel" was good, and intentional as I changed the type of action before it scared or irritated her. The "timing" part of the equation was accidental, giving her less passivity than she wanted while still using passivity to help her pause, rest, and remember our most important moments together. Each pause we took in harmony was so sweet, so breathtakingly fulfilling, both of us wanted more.

Yet…I could feel the end of the year breathing down my neck already.

My good timing that first week was accidental and motivated poorly. We were sprinting from success to success, and I was getting greedier with every win.

↓ Myrnah was a monumentally generous soul.

Understanding Concern, Curiosity, and Comfort

By Week Two, I had built such a desire for harmony through timing in Myrnah that I was now able to use it as a reward, particularly when Myrnah was eating hay or grazing in the small grass area of the paddock.

I am not going to lie to you, withholding harmony deliberately and then using it as a reward was pushing the moral edge of the rules I had set for the experiment, and this was a flaw in the process I would later regret. At the time, I was doing the best I knew how to do with a limited perspective and a narrow window of awareness.

From a lifetime of hating dominance-driven training but not knowing any other option, I had learned to paint it with pretty words—to pretend force wasn't really force and the end justified the means. So there I was at the beginning of my project, the project that was supposed to change all that, and I was falling into old habits already. I may not have been feeding Myrnah out of my hand, or threatening her with rope, stick, or entrapment, but I was withholding the harmony I had taught her to love until she tried a little harder to do what I wanted.

Yes, in comparison to the training I had done before, it was "better"... in a morally gray way.

Myrnah was free to walk away if she didn't like what I wanted her to do, and if she had, I would have gone back a step in the process to developing her love of harmony with me. But she didn't. Myrnah was a monumentally generous soul and seemed predominantly curious about what I would ask for next.

This gave me the license to ask too much.

What is "too much" when training in freedom? I will answer as honestly as I know how, from experience hard-won.

You have asked too much when horses start to use their bodies more than they are using their brains, their senses, and their awareness.

Let me demonstrate this with an example: I had a desperate desire to teach Myrnah to follow me. The way I taught this behavior was:

1. I taught her to want more time in harmony with me.

2. I taught her she could get some time in harmony with me if she touched my hand.

3. I held that hand just out of reach, so she had to take a step to touch it.

4. The distances got wider, so she had to take more steps to reach the target of my hand.

5. I drew away from her so the target was moving, and she had to follow it before she could touch it.

This is a fairly standard training procedure, and at the time I was proud of myself for managing it without tools. It felt like success—a success I would later regret. I glossed over in my mind that Myrnah's choices hadn't really been made in freedom.

Now, in hindsight, I know this wasn't really training in freedom from the way Myrnah's curiosity dimmed with every repetition. Her ears became more and more still, listening to the world less, and her eyes glazed over a bit. She would follow me as I asked her to achieve the peace we both wanted, but her senses participated less and less, and then not at all anymore. Our practice was becoming more and more of *a means to an end* for both of us, and the end goal of "having a horse follow you without thought" is short-sighted at best, even if the horse is following you to achieve the feeling of harmony you both want.

Freedom is about awareness—the awareness to make the choices that are right for the self, first, and then hopefully for the partnership as well.

I was fumbling my way through a process that would ultimately teach me to train the horse's *emotional system* first, *mental system* second, and *physical system* third.

When you train horses' *emotional systems*, you allow and encourage them to *feel* things. You know when they are feeling things by observing the use of their five senses. When horses make a good focus change (move from noticing one thing to noticing a different thing), you synchronize with the horse and stop adding information to the situation. Their senses have been stimulated in a way that *regulates their stress positively*, and you physically acknowledge it and then give the horse's brain time to process the positive feeling. To *regulate positively* does not always mean *lower* stress; it means to raise or lower as desired. Raising stress heightens awareness, and lowering stress allows the horse to rest. When first training with an emotional focus, regulation will be accidental. With practice, it will become habitual, and with mastery it will become a choice with multiple good options horses can make for themselves.

When you train horses' *mental systems*, you show them how they can do one thing to

> *We must learn to treat emotional training just like we do physical muscular training: it needs both exercise and rest to be effective.*

get another thing, because life is sometimes transactional.

When you train horses' *physical systems*, you move their bodies in repetitions so they become habituated and stronger in the ways you prefer.

We must learn to treat emotional training just like we do physical muscular training: it needs both exercise and rest to be effective. The exercise is those focus changes I mentioned—noticing one thing and then noticing a different thing. When this exercise of noticing, feeling, and thinking catches the attention of a friend (me), who responds by switching from action to passivity, it can be felt by the horse more fully.

To make a human analogy, when we experience something good, the first thing we want to do is tell a friend about it or share it with

/ PART II / *Gathering Inspiration from Experience*

Myrnah often gave me grace when I wanted too much; she had understanding to spare until I developed my own.

/ * see page 58 /

someone. *It is the sharing of the experience that intensifies the feeling of the experience.* However, when we share the experience and our friend insists on talking over us or sharing their story at the same time, the intensity of the feeling is lost. When we share a feeling with someone we value, they need to show us they are aware *while being passive enough to allow us the full extent of enjoyment.* This give-and-take of shared feelings is what builds relationships, and more importantly, what builds *emotional fitness* and *emotional stability* in the individuals in the relationship. *Emotional fitness* is the ability to choose a focus that promotes *harmony and cooperation* over a focus that is *exciting or habitual.* Emotional fitness is gained through alternating exercising focus changes* and rest. *Emotional stability* is the ability to hold one focus for longer without becoming overwhelmed. Emotional fitness becomes emotional stability with practice.

For horses, emotional fitness and stability is built from having friends who notice:

★ when they need help changing focus and offer potentially different things to think about.

★ and respond with a switch from active to passive when focus changes are good. (Remember: A *good* focus change is one that causes the use of the senses in stress-regulating ways—not all focus changes are good.)

★ when the brain is tired from the focus change exercises and needs a pause to process the things learned.

This means that horses being trained emotionally first in freedom have three needs:

★ *Concern*—the need for activity or distraction; if a friend doesn't offer help, the horse will create the activity themselves.

★ *Curiosity*—the need for passivity, someone to notice, witness, and share feelings in harmony.

★ *Comfort*—the need for a pause in sensation to process the learning that came before.

Addressing these three needs is how we train emotionally first.

In Week Two with Myrnah, I had jumped ahead to the mental and the physical training priorities, and my timing was falling out of sync from Myrnah's.

The Gift of Refocusing Pressure

By the fourth week of my experiment, a necessity had come up that thankfully forced me back toward putting emotional training first. This necessity was Myrnah's second round of vaccinations.

After gathering wild horses off the land in the American West, the Bureau of Land Management (BLM) deworms and vaccinates all Mustangs before sending them to adoptive homes. I had received special dispensation to be able to take Myrnah after her first round of vaccinations but before her second ones, by promising I would get them done myself.

I was terrified.

Not of the needle or of the activity—I had done things like give animals vaccines before. I also wasn't scared of the training preparation I needed to do prior. What I did fear was the lack of control I was going to have during the vaccination process. In my experience, a lack of control led to horses getting scared, and scared horses were willing to hurt others to save themselves.

How was I going to make sure I could accomplish the task without scaring Myrnah? The needle I needed to stick in her neck suddenly seemed huge!

I was going to ask Myrnah to stand in the middle of the paddock, without a fence to trap her against, without a halter to focus her, without food to direct her thoughts or soothe her potential anxiety. This interaction between us could potentially color the way she thought of me, shading our entire relationship with associations of distrust. I couldn't let that happen.

Was it possible it could go well? Yes. Was I confident I could set us up for success? No.

My hands were shaking as I had never felt them shake as I unpacked the syringe my veterinarian had prepared for me to give Myrnah.

↓ Could I refocus Myrnah toward things that soothed her when I needed to?

/ PART II / *Gathering Inspiration from Experience*

↓ Resting and remembering our emotional success and the positive associations was the key.

From the moment I'd made the promise at the corrals in Oregon, I'd found myself cursing the additional time pressure it put on us. Myrnah and I were supposed to have a relationship built on trust—gradually and naturally occurring trust—built slowly through a million tiny experiences. The vaccination process felt like too much too soon, but it was the cost I'd had to pay to bring Myrnah home. Now, there was no way around it.

How could I set Myrnah up to be brave, to be curious, and to regulate her emotions if the situation began to feel overwhelming to her? The physical preparation for the act of being vaccinated was the easy part. I taught her to yield her nose to the left or the right from my fingertips on the outside of her face, bending her neck around me. Then, after the neck bend, I reinforced that physical movement with an invitation to soften the muscles in her neck (so a needle could slide in painlessly) by spending time together in passive harmony as we both now loved. Gradually I added a pre-cue sensation of tapping, pinching, or twisting the skin where the needle might need to go in to link the increased softening of the neck muscles around the eventual pressure of the needle.

Without a halter for support, I needed to build an emotional foundation for this physical process.

Emotions motivate horses to either cooperate or defend themselves. When horses focus on something upsetting or overwhelming, they will feel increasingly motivated to defend themselves. When horses focus on something that stimulates the senses without crossing the threshold of overwhelm, their curiosity will motivate them to cooperate and explore more of that feeling.

Emotions run in predictable patterns given the stimuli and the memory of what emotions the specific stimuli may have triggered in the horse previously. We cannot always control the emotions a horse feels, or the stimuli that trigger those emotions, but we *can* impact how the horse remembers the situation. We do that through how *we* participate. Horses are herd animals, and this means how the herd responds has a huge impact on how their memories are stored. When horses use their senses and feel an emotion, there will always be a small part of their brain that notices if another member of the herd also feels it or if they are all alone in that experience. When an experience is shared with another, without distraction, it is far more powerfully remembered.

To use this in training, we can use a progression of reinforcement. (Reinforcement in this case is simply acknowledgment of an experience and related emotion and then passivity in harmony with the horse, because the

/ * see page 58 /
/ * see page 76 /

true reinforcer is the feeling that is experienced without distraction.) Feelings are caused by the activation of the senses, and the activation of the senses is caused by a change of focus from one thing to another thing. The better horses get at focus changes*, the more reinforced they will feel for behaviors linked to those feelings in the future.

In training, our *focus-change goals* must start with a low-enough intensity that the horse's emotional system does not become overwhelmed before it has gained fitness through exercise and rest. We also must be willing to retreat back to less-intense goals when the horse's emotional system becomes tired.

Consider this list of focus-change goals:

1. Small focus changes (the flick of an ear or the change of an eye).

2. Category changes (I explain navigating these categories—*Self, Herd, Environment, Leader, Learning**).

3. Specific category changes (skipping over responses to the categories that are easy, stretching for those that are more of a challenge).

4. Drawing focus changes (when you look at something, your horse should copy you).

5. Maintaining one focus (ask your horse to hold focus on something important and take action every time the horse tries to think about something different).

If "1" is coming easily, we stop reinforcing it and only reinforce "2." When "2" is coming easily, we stop reinforcing it, as well, and only reinforce "3," and so on. Gradually the horse needs to make bigger and bigger efforts to get our attention and so develops a wider range of optional ways to regulate emotions.

When we progress through this list too quickly, the horse will not feel emotionally strong enough to make the change needed to regulate stress and find harmony. Frustration may cause the horse to get defensive, showing *more* fight and flight instead of less.

This theory of training the emotional system by using focus changes, and thus enabling emotional regulation in the horse, can be understood in this way: When focusing on one thing is causing emotional dysregulation (which leads to the internal discomfort that precedes physical fight or flight), horses can choose to change focus to something different that *lowers* stress,

↓ Sometimes, the slightest flick of the ear to catch a sound is a focus change worth pausing to remember.

A habit of focus choices that lead to cooperative behavior is the goal.

or they can choose to double down on the focus that will likely motivate defensive behavior. The goal is that "cooperate" or "defend" becomes a choice horses are capable of making because they have practiced enough focus changes that they *know* they have the capability to focus in the way they would like to rather than in the way that may be simply reactionary.

As I learned from Ransom, when horses can get the attention of their herd by changing the group's focus to a stimulant of a more comfortable feeling, and as long as they are safe enough, they will choose the more comfortable option (cooperation rather than defensiveness). However, horses need enough practice making such choices that they learn it is always an option. The more they practice cooperative thinking and have it reinforced by the herd (with passivity and harmony), the stronger that skill of focus change becomes, and then the skill turns into a habit. The stronger the habit of cooperative thinking becomes, the more the horse can explore possible options, including what might be "better," when faced with a decision.

The thing is, we also *do* want horses to be able to concentrate on one thing *without* changing focus because they can learn things faster that way, but this only applies when they feel safe enough to not get defensive. The problem with building a habit of "hyperfocus" is that it *can* lead to overwhelm and defensive behavior, creating a self-fulfilling prophecy for horses—*because they ran, or because they fought, they survived*; they have no evidence that they would have survived if they had chosen to change focus and "feel better" by finding harmony instead.

As good partners, it becomes our job to show horses evidence that changing focus to "feel better" is safe and worth repeating when they feel their stress rising to overwhelming levels.

In the case of the vaccinations, I needed Myrnah to skillfully regulate her stress and only think about the things that made her willing to cooperate with the situation. My physical goal of having her move or hold her body in the right way was not enough; she needed her feelings to motivate cooperation between us, no matter *what* happened physically.

When it came time to give her the vaccination, I was as prepared as I thought I could be, and we had the cameras rolling. Hopefully, Myrnah would learn through the event that she could trust me and was safe (enough) in my company; if not, I could study the film footage as many times as necessary to help me figure out where I had gone wrong.

My hands on the syringe were shaking and clumsy, my vision was a little blurry, and it was hard to breathe. *I wanted so desperately to get this right*. I played by the rules I had made for myself, pausing to breathe in harmony with Myrnah whenever she chose to focus on things that clearly made her more curious, not less. I responded with all the right timing in the ways we had practiced, but that day *I* was different—so very different from the way I normally behaved. Luckily for me, Myrnah hadn't experienced any bad situations where people with shaking, clumsy hands and blurry vision made her unsafe or uncomfortable, so she leaned into the curiosity my different behavior created in her. She nuzzled my hair and breathed on me, soothing me in every way she knew how.

I fumbled with the syringe and did all the actions wrong a few times before I finally set the needle in her neck correctly and pushed the plunger. My awkwardness was okay, though, because, for the most part, I got the timing right. I just kept moving through the stages of the process that might scare Myrnah, and they were over before there was a chance of overwhelm. Around the main event, I reinforced and helped her remember as many good moments related to her focus change and curiosity as possible.

We achieved an important milestone together, and I wanted more moments like it!

↓ Myrnah wanted more demonstrations of understanding—understanding of how she felt.

Feel and Timing

At my stage of learning about a month into the project, I still didn't understand that *timing* was more important than *feel*— feel being what helps you determine *what* to do; timing being *when* you do it.

I knew timing was important, but I was still stuck on tangible goals of "how many tasks I could ask Myrnah to accomplish with me." I was focused on "what" we did together. Every day I asked her for a few more yields and a few more follows. *A few more...a few more...a few more...a few more...*

Repetitions might strengthen a physical skill, but when repetitions are prioritized over timing, you leave the horse wanting less and less of that activity.

It seemed I had the first part of the training in freedom right, but after that, Myrnah and I were at an impasse. The more actions I pushed Myrnah to do in repetition, the more she craved harmony, and that was good... but then what? I wanted more demonstrations of skills; Myrnah wanted more demonstrations of understanding—understanding of how she felt and how those feelings were always changing in cycles and patterns.

Continuing to train in the best way I knew how at that time, I would ask for a physical skill (a yielding movement away from me or a drawing movement toward me) and when she did it right, I would pause to help her remember that success. The problem was, often the repetitive task I was giving Myrnah was causing her to think less, feel less, and be less motivated. This was not because it was the wrong action, but simply because I was asking at the wrong time and ending at the wrong time. But I didn't know what I didn't know at that point, and Myrnah wasn't sure how to explain it to me. Gradually her expression became more and more disinterested. She allowed me to keep pushing for my goals, while she tuned me out more and more.

I had been taught all my life that relaxation in horses was a good thing. A deep breath or a yawn was a sign a training session was going well. I now know this is a huge oversimplification, and a few more factors, such as what happens *after* that sign of relaxation, need to be considered before deciding if it is a sign that training is going well.

It never occurred to me that horses might fake a yawn if they were rewarded consistently enough for it, and it took me a very long time to realize Myrnah had figured out a loophole in my training plan. If she really wanted harmony and flow and passivity from me, all she needed to do was yawn and keep yawning while I got quiet, mentally patting myself on the back for a job well done.

It wasn't until the weather started to get colder and most horses had visible breath streaming out like little dragons, that I realized Myrnah wasn't yawning like the other horses. She was simply opening her mouth a lot around me.

She was pretending to yawn.

I had been taught that witnessing signs of relaxation was a good thing in horse training because horse training is often an activity fraught with stress and tension, and relaxation is a powerful contrast to that. Successful training is all about contrast—the bigger the contrast between two states, the more memorable the experience becomes. You need both parts of a contrast to train effectively. Formerly, I had learned to use some sort of pressure (often one that caused a negative feeling, like discomfort) to motivate a behavior or action in a horse and then the contrast of relaxation to make it memorable.

Relaxation isn't a *feeling* state; it is a *non-feeling* state. The more relaxed horses become, the more they quiet their sensory awareness, feeling less and less in the moment and allowing the full facilities of memory to solidify the learning that came before.

When dominance-based training is used, it is the withholding of food or the threat of pressure that shapes a horse's physical behaviors. A good trainer does this with artistic subtlety; a bad trainer does it with a cascade of abuse. In either case, relaxation afterward will enhance the horse's memories of what was learned from that experience—for example, "the faster you touch the target the faster the food is delivered," or "the more immediately you step forward when you feel the pressure of the halter, the faster it is released."

I was attempting to do something different than this typical training methodology, and it wasn't going well, because I didn't know exactly

/ * see page 99 /

Successful training

is all about contrast—the bigger the contrast between two states, the more memorable the experience becomes. You need both parts of a contrast to train effectively.

how to replace contrast with subtlety yet. I was trying to allow Myrnah to feel her own positive emotional states of curiosity in contrast to the relaxation of non-feeling (states of comfort or relaxation). I was finding this could be quietly effective, but it seemed I couldn't stop slipping back into the old patterns of dominance. And I knew dominance was not going to work because I didn't have the tools to support it, so our interactions degraded into a messy power struggle of "insistent leadership."* When you try to force horses to do things they don't want to do without the right tools, the relationship gets worse, not better.

For example, I kept trying to use the pressure of my fingertips the way I knew how to use the pressure of a halter or rope and then contrast that with relaxation, but it didn't work. And I kept trying to use the pressure of my actions around the horse to stimulate her desire for harmony. This worked for a while, but ultimately, I did too much repetition without good timing, and then Myrnah wanted to ignore me more than she wanted to interact with me.

In this mess of failed timing and ineffective dominance, Myrnah learned she could get my attention and my passivity with relaxation—even when she didn't feel relaxed, she could get it with a whole series of fake yawns, which had me fooled.

I know now that the moments when Myrnah showed the curiosity and internal positive feelings I wanted were when I should have paused and been passive. That was the important part!

/ PART II / *Gathering Inspiration from Experience*

↓ ↘ The completion of physical tasks stroked my ego and made me feel like we were making progress, but that wasn't the important dimension of progress. Myrnah would need to show me again and again: how we feel is more important than what we do.

Yet my impatience made me rush right past the feelings and immediately try to pressure feelings into the actions that I thought I wanted more. In hindsight, I am profoundly embarrassed how often I slipped back into my old training patterns and how often Myrnah had to help me correct my course.

Here is the truth I have discovered: training with too much pressure, or making *actions* more important than *feelings*, is a losing game unless you have a horse trapped—either by an addiction to the food you hold control over, or by a fence or rope. Take away the entrapment factor and eventually, you will need to learn a different way to train. If you resist it as I did, the horse simply walks away, hides behind another horse, or learns better and better ways to ignore you and pacify you with as little effort as possible.

When you want the horse to put effort into training with you, *emotional training* must maintain priority. This means:

★ Being passive when the horse is most curious, interested, and engaged.

★ Being active or asking the horse to be active when you think you can improve feelings of curiosity.

★ Being passive when the horse finds comfort and feels less, remembering a moment of curiosity.

I was getting this all wrong, and the donkey-like expression on Myrnah's face was showing up more often, letting me know something had to change. In this case, my ego was the catalyst. I would love to say it was my wisdom or my Zen-like search for peace…but that would be a lie. It was my desire for us to look better in pictures.

Cameras love emotion. All those moments of no emotion or lack of feeling lead to a lot of pictures being discarded.

Filming was continuous throughout my project, and each week, still pictures were also taken for my ongoing blog posts about the experience. This meant that each week, I was confronted by evidence that I was doing something wrong, as I viewed video and photographs where Myrnah looked less and less interested in everything.

How could I fix it? Timing of course!

I needed to get better at being passive in the few moments Myrnah was interested in something, anything! And learning more about the things Myrnah might be interested in was a key turning point in my understanding. In this effort, I broke the horse's curiosity into five *focus categories*:

★ Self

★ Herd

★ Environment

★ Leader

★ Learning

An acronym is an easy way to remember these categories: when you take the first letter of each category and put them together, it spells SHELL, and the awareness of all five categories in balance is what helps horses feel safe, like they have a shell of protective awareness.

/ * see page 98 /

- *Self-focus* looks like ears out to the side, eyes a little glazed over, awareness of sensations inside the body instead of outside the body. Self-focus is a curious state in its first moments. Horses check in with themselves: "How do I feel about this situation?"

- *Herd-focus* looks like horses paying attention to and listening to anyone they might communicate with. Horse, human, dog, cat, it depends on individual horses and how far they think their herd extends. Herd-focus is a curious state in its first moments. Horses check to see how everyone else is feeling.

- *Environment-focus* looks like horses paying attention to and listening to anything around them that they will not communicate with. Environment-focus is a curious state in its first few moments. Horses check to see how safe they are in their surroundings.

- *Leader-focus* looks like horses listening to and looking at anyone whose decisions they are currently in harmony with. (There are many ways to be a leader or a decision-maker that I will go into later.*) Leader-focus is a curious state in its first few moments. Horses check to adapt their harmony to the leader's decisions.

- *Learning-focus* looks like an intensification of any of the other four categories. Learning about the self might be a big deep breath, a lick of the lips, a chew, or a yawn. Learning about the herd or the environment or the leader might be looking at it from different perspectives—from up high, down low, out of the right eye, out of the left eye—or smelling with one nostril and then the other. The learning focus is an active use of the senses in multiple ways about one subject. Learning-focus is curiosity perpetuated because it involves constantly changing focus in small ways.

When any of the first four categories of focus are held for longer than a few moments, they stop being curious states because there is no new information being added. The longer a focus is held, the closer it becomes to some sort of mental and emotional rest.

Since I am being honest, I will admit that at this point in the training with Myrnah, I just wanted to be able to take good pictures. I wasn't thinking about how safe she felt, or how curiosity would lead to more motivation to do things with me. The fact that my physical goal lined up with her emotional needs was purely accidental. With my photogenic hopes in mind, the best possible choice of focus category for Myrnah was going to be the environment. When Myrnah looked out at the horizon far away, her ears would prick forward and her neck would arch a little. This was beautiful; this is what I needed to mark and capture and help her remember…so I could get better photographs.

I laugh now at the irony: My ego wanting to make faster and faster progress with the skills of yields and draw, and through that killing all the motivation Myrnah had for doing the work with me. Then my ego wanting to look good on camera saving us both, bringing light, joy, and enthusiasm back into our experiences together.

> *The more aware Myrnah became of the world around her, the safer she felt, and the safer she felt, the better she could rest, and the better she could rest, the more she could remember what she had focused on to feel safe.*

Myrnah started to develop a stronger and stronger association where *cameras equated with environment-focus*. The camera also caught touching moments when Myrnah looked at me as we fell into harmony, moments she noticed the other horses adjusting around us, or moments she needed to know more about a sight, a sound, or a smell and was in a learning mode. Since those moments made good pictures too, I learned to reinforce them. (I did have the most consistent response of passivity when Myrnah looked at the environment, though, because that was the look I loved most.)

When I say I *reinforced* these states, I simply mean I made time to rest in passive harmony after them, in order to solidify the memory of feelings linked to events, as we've already discussed. Rest does two things: it helps a horse remember the feeling that came before, and it gathers energy for the next change, which might be *emotional, mental,* or *physical*—or all three at once. When horses work *cooperatively*, they separate the three states, with the *emotional feeling* helping them decide what is important, the *mental thought* helping them decide how best to get what is important, and the *physical action* working with others to succeed toward that goal. When horses work *defensively* all three states tend to happen together: the feeling triggers a knee-jerk thought solution and the body acts on it. This kind of operation is very unpredictable and difficult to be in harmony with because the goal of defense is to separate from others.

(As herd animals, horses have different levels of defense and unpredictability, depending on whether they are trying to separate from a "danger" outside the herd and stay with the herd or if they are trying to separate from other herd mates.)

Over time, I was finding the solution to defensive behavior in horses was to spend more time reinforcing feelings of safety, which came from awareness of all five focus categories. Or, when horses were not developed enough to be aware for themselves, they came from a dependency on *others* who were aware of all five categories.

I am in awe still that life allowed Myrnah and me this meandering path of discovery. One that allowed me to be so clueless and ego-driven and somehow stumble into the right answers anyway. The more aware Myrnah became of the world around her, the safer she felt, and the safer she felt, the better she could rest, and the better she could rest, the more she could remember what she had focused on to feel safe. And because of all this, the more cooperative she naturally became.

Cooperation is a two-way street though. If Myrnah showed me her willingness to cooperate would it strengthen my ability to do so, too?

↓ Myrnah was an amazing problem-solver and learned the patterns quickly. Then I could draw her into self focus and rest by demonstrating it for her to copy.

/ * see page 76 /

Feeling Safe Enough

For a while Myrnah's cooperative tendencies washed over me like a flood of peace I couldn't help but melt into.

In Week Five the priority became hoof trimming, as I wanted Myrnah to stay comfortable on her feet. The miles she traveled each day had diminished greatly from what she was accustomed to in the wild. Without the wear and tear of repeated movement over abrasive ground, the use of a handheld rasp was our friend…if we could just get the timing right.

I had established that my actions around Myrnah were intended to cause curiosity, focus changes, and an awareness of the focus categories that made her feel safer. It was good in theory. Slowly, I became better in my timing so that *practice matched theory.*

With handling her feet in mind, my actions consisted of approaching Myrnah, stroking her neck, stroking her shoulder, stroking her leg, rocking her knee joint forward so it could relax back, stepping away, and repeating again. These were all intended to stimulate feeling and awareness. It was important that I alternated different actions before any of them irritated her to the point of pulling away or pushing into me. It was also important that I kept playing at my various actions until she found the focus category I hoped she would focus on (which was any category that made her feel safer within her shell of awareness*). Then we could pause, my passivity allowing her to rest and remember the information she had gathered through her curiosity related to my actions.

Myrnah was an amazing problem-solver and learned the patterns quickly. Then we could progress to using draw to change focus. If I looked and listened to the focus category I wanted her to pay attention to, would she copy me? If not, I would go back a step to using various actions around her to cause focus changes until she found the right one.

Learning to rest on three feet was a skill that expedited the necessities of hoof trimming.

Then it was time to try the ultimate goal: holding one focus.

As I explained earlier, holding one focus is how horses learn the fastest, so it is the first thing most training methods attempt to develop. Holding one focus intensifies learning while challenging a horse's natural instincts to be aware more broadly. It is in the contrast of these ideals that horses become the best versions of themselves.

The first natural situation where these ideals are challenged is between the waking and sleeping states—waking being more aware, sleeping being a holding of one focus. Horses sleep differently from humans. While humans are designed to sleep for eight hours without moving, horses are designed to sleep for short durations, waking often to check their state of safety before resting again. Each period of rest is a test of how safe a horse feels, and quality is more valuable than quantity. Quality is determined by how cooperative the horse feels upon waking and before resting again.

Somehow Myrnah and I again accidentally slid into this theory when it came to trimming her hooves. I played with alternating actions—my actions around her and actions I asked *her* to take—until we found a focus category that was good for her feeling of safety at that moment. We knew the focus category was good for her by two criteria: Had she checked each category recently enough to feel safe? And which focus categories did she have the best past associations with in situations like this? Then we would rest

↓ This prioritizing of a physical goal over an emotional one was one of my many failures dressed up as a temporary success.

with that focus for a breath or two before finding the next good focus change for her.

Eventually, all the focus changes as she shifted her curiosity made Myrnah's brain tired, and I could feel her wanting to rest in self-focus. In a perfect world, I would have assessed how good the feelings were preceding the rest and possibly just rested with her to solidify the best memories of working together. But in my imperfect world, I needed to get her feet trimmed, so when she was ready to rest, I would pick up a foot and allow her to rest standing on three feet. This normalized the feeling of standing on three feet at a time when feelings were low in intensity, so Myrnah was less likely to remember any timing mistakes I might make

It felt so very good to get the first hoof trim finished.

during the hoof-trimming process.

The most important part, though, was putting down that foot and going back into action around her *before she rested too long*. Resting too long leaves a horse feeling unsafe with a tendency to defensive actions (like pulling the foot out of my hand). So, I needed to take action proactively and wake Myrnah up a little *before* she felt unsafe, while her brain would still return to full awareness in a cooperative way. Once she was a little curious and cooperative, I could let her fall back asleep and resume the practice of holding up a hoof for the right amount of time.

Slowly I added one or two strokes of the rasp, or a little rocking of the foot left or right before putting the foot down and going into action around her to trigger curiosity. Then the rasping or the foot rocking became enough to trigger a little curiosity without me having to put the foot down, so Myrnah felt safe and could fall asleep again. With practice, I could keep the foot up for longer and longer as she came in and out of sleep gracefully.

Enough focus changes to keep her feeling safe; enough rest to soothe her tired brain before it got defensive. I didn't always get the timing right, but I got it right more than I got it wrong, and little by little her feet became trimmed and tidy.

I wish with all my heart my training experiement held a course like this for the rest of the year, and that I always got the timing more right than wrong…but that is not how this story goes.

/ * see page 76 /

A Horse's Hierarchy of Needs

In Week Six I got impatient again. I wanted more physical evidence of progress, and I thought being able to move at faster speeds would provide proof. Myrnah was not interested in going faster anywhere. My problem was not her problem.

We must remember that Myrnah was three or four years old. Birthdates are not recorded out in the wild, so I could only guess at her age. There was also a high likelihood Myrnah was pregnant, though I was not yet sure of that. She had been starved from the lack of food and water available on the range her herd was from—this I could see with my own eyes and feel with my fingers as I traced the bones protruding where they should not have been visible.

Myrnah now had all the food and water she could want, available to her 24/7, a good friend in Cleo to help keep her safe, and ample opportunities to rest. I thought that providing for these needs should be enough to "crack on" with our training together, but Myrnah had other ideas.

Horses have a *hierarchy of needs* that starts with their basics: *food, water, rest,* and *friends*. There is an essential level of these they will attempt to secure, even before considering safety. As soon as that essential level is achieved, they will take a quick assessment of their safety, and when that is good enough, they will consider their social needs.

The horse's hierarchy of needs looks like this:

/ A / *Basic* (enough food, water, rest, and friends).

/ B / *Safety* (awareness of self, herd, environment, leader, and learning—see the focus categories*).

↓ When I got the timing wrong, Myrnah had no interest in working with me.

/ C / *Companionship* (the horse showing others their interests in harmony).

/ D / *Entertainment* (the horse taking part in someone else's interests).

The *basic needs* are the foundation. Horses will simply grab a bite of food or a quick drink of water whenever they can, even if they feel a bit unsafe. They will gravitate closer to other animals in their instinctual herding way, regardless if it is safe for them to do so or not.

When Myrnah felt pushed too far beyond her hierarchy of needs, defensive behaviors became increasingly apparent.

They will shut down their senses and rest their brain from time to time, wherever they may be and whatever the weather. All of this, horses will do thoughtlessly if need be and before they prioritize other things. Without a feeling of safety, the quality of their basic needs might not be good, but they will reach for the basic needs first anyway.

It is only after horses start to feel a little *safe*, though, through the use of their five senses to check their five focus categories (or trusting a herd mate to do so for them), that their basic needs can be filled with quality, not just quantity. When feeling safe, the food can be chosen with care, the water can be savored, the friends can be chosen to support the creation of more safe feelings, and the rests taken can be deeper.

With basic needs and safety attended to, *social needs* have room to evolve—first through horses showing others what they are interested in (*getting* attention), and then through horses being interested in what others find interesting (*giving* attention).

Training in freedom, I found I could encourage Myrnah to focus on the needs hierarchy level one stage beyond where she was inclined, in alternation with the level she thought was important at the time. When I got the timing right, showing Myrnah that I understood her hierarchy of needs, she became more and more curious about the next level of development.

↓ Friends were every bit as important to Myrnah as rest and food.

When I pushed too far, too fast, Myrnah got defensive.

At this point, you can probably guess I had to try pushing too far, too fast first.

Myrnah wanted to eat, sleep, and pay attention to her friends. She was good-natured about practicing focus changes and becoming more aware of how safe she was, as long as we could go back to the basic needs frequently.

I wanted her to follow me, which as I've shared, we had worked on early in our time together. But by Week Six, walking wasn't good

/ * see page 76 /

enough anymore, I wanted her to run after me with bursts of enthusiasm and joy!

My efforts to make this happen backfired. Myrnah's strong self-focus started turning more and more into looks of self-defense, irritation, and moments of aggression.

I would run around, trying to demonstrate the joy and enthusiasm for speed I wanted her to show also. Myrnah would frustratedly try to catch me to nuzzle me with her soft nose and coax me into harmony with her again. But I wouldn't let her catch me until she was willing to take just a step or two of faster walk, or maybe even a step of trot. I could withhold the "carrot" of harmony until she put a little more effort into speed, but there was not enough freedom in that choice for her to do it willingly. It was a minimal effort made under duress.

I was learning that there was a lot of gray area between taking away all my tools and training with a full sense of freedom. I guess I had to cross that line of freedom again and again and again to fully understand where it was. Each time I crossed it with my training and caused Myrnah to feel worse instead of better, I found myself sitting in the hay in their paddock late at night, listening to the horses chewing, crying my eyes out, and apologizing for all the things I didn't understand yet. The mares alternated between eating and nuzzling my tear-stained cheeks. This was a problem they could solve with me, enough food, enough water, enough friends, and enough rest. And I cried in their company until all the tears were gone, went back to bed exhausted and hopeless, then woke up in the morning, more determined than ever to figure it out.

I didn't know until later, I was missing an important understanding of the horse's hierarchy of needs.

/ A / *Basic* (enough food, water, rest, and friends).

/ B / *Safety* (awareness of self, herd, environment, leader, and learning—see the focus categories*).

/ C / *Companionship* (the horse showing others their interests in harmony).

/ D / *Entertainment* (the horse taking part in someone else's interests).

I understood A and B, but I had no clue how important C was, and I was pushing way too hard for D.

The Forest Holds Understanding

Not knowing what to do, I retreated to the solution of my childhood: more time in the forest.

Myrnah and I walked and walked and walked through the woods together. We walked as slowly as she wanted to go, with many breaks for her to address her basic needs.

It was clear I was getting nowhere by trying to push my agenda on Myrnah. If I continued to persist, I knew it wouldn't be long before I needed a halter or a fence to keep her near me. I needed to stop irritating her before we reached that point. So, we retreated several steps, and I listened to Myrnah instead of the clock ticking.

On our walks, she would graze for a bit; I would ask her to change focus, and then reinforce it with many moments of passivity, encouraging her to go back to addressing her basic needs.

Horses and humans share an interesting contrarian nature in one key factor that training depends on. *We can only want more of something we don't have enough of.* What determines not enough? We were enjoying it when it ended and so we are left wanting more.

When I retreated to walk through the forests and meadows with Myrnah, first I allowed her to fill her basic needs fully in my company, to a point that it seemed she was feeling less interested in that and resting more, which I knew would be naturally followed by a desire for more awareness. I would ask her to change focus at a time when it was easy and natural for her to do so and then encourage her to go back to her basic needs at a moment when she was most enjoying being aware of the world around her and her safety in it.

With repetitions, Myrnah desired more and more to look at the world and be curious. This curiosity led to a desire to go see things that she

↓ With repetitions, Myrnah desired more and more to look at the world and be curious.

↓ Companionship was allowing Myrnah to show me all the things that were important to her.

noticed. We moved from seeing things far away to investigating them from closer viewpoints, and she took me with her on these voyages of discovery.

This was the stage of the hierarchy I hadn't paid enough attention to: *companionship*.

My job was simply to stay in harmony with Myrnah as her companion, maintaining whatever position I had been passively holding at the standstill as Myrnah eased us into walk and took us to look around the next tree, investigate the next rock, or smell the next slug we found,

↓ In valuing Myrnah's interests, we built the foundation for all our future entertainments.

sliming its way across the pungent earth. Then at her peak of enjoyment (sensory awareness), I would encourage Myrnah to walk back to the barn, eat a little more hay, get some water, or take a nap in my company to solve the basic need problems before they had been neglected for too long.

When I took responsibility for helping Myrnah remember the foundation of our problems to solve—the basic needs—that freed her up to push me to acknowledge the higher-level problems of safety, companionship, and eventually, entertainment. In understanding the hierarchy of needs, my job was to *limit* Myrnah just enough that she wanted *more* learning, instead of pushing her so hard that she wanted *less* learning.

My goal was to teach Myrnah all the things domestic horses knew how to do, including carrying a rider. All those skills fell in the hierarchical category of *entertainment* for her though. These are the needs horses don't know yet, the novelty of things they haven't even thought of. But before entertainment came the very important element of *companionship*, allowing Myrnah to show me all the things *she* wanted to learn about, in my company. Then we came back again and again to the basic foundation that supported that growth.

This is how *intrinsic* motivation is nurtured. By having not quite enough of something while still having some choice in the matter.

As we've discussed, most training relies heavily upon pressure applied from the outside of the horse to motivate learning. Even food rewards are based on the pressure of lack and the release of that lack when the food is delivered by the human. This is a focus on *extrinsic* motivation, when all the pressure or lack of pressure is controlled by someone else.

What I was attempting to do was to access and shape Myrnah's intrinsic motivation: doing things because of how she felt inside her body; helping her have the power to change the way she felt to motivate herself. When horses know they will feel one way looking at one thing but have the choice to look at another thing that makes them feel another way, this gives them the power to motivate different actions, depending on what they focus on.

My goal was to use the timing of my passivity to point out Myrnah's own power to choose, because choosing what felt most important to her was her freedom. But to complicate matters, I wanted to train her to have habits of thoughtful cooperation. I wanted her to feel free to make the choices that were right for her, but I also wanted her to feel good more than she felt bad. It was my belief that habits of defense felt bad to a herd animal, and habits of voluntary cooperation felt good. By encouraging Myrnah to go back to solving her basic needs problems before she was ready, I could develop intrinsic motivation for more learning and also foster both the end goals— freedom of choice and cooperative thinking.

Yes, yes…there is an elephant in the room I need to address.

Intrinsic and extrinsic motivation is not black and white, there are many shades of gray, and I was experimenting with them all. I also acknowledge that my motivation for helping Myrnah was ultimately self-serving. Developing a horse partner who could think for herself, make good choices, emotionally self-regulate, and feel motivated to learn with me, while being free, sounded too good to be true. But if it was possible, I wanted that unicorn.

↓ I could only learn to shape Myrnah's intrinsic motivations if I learned more about them first.

Leadership Options

When it comes to training horses, wanting too much too soon seems to be the root of all evil.

As soon as I had one skill solid with Myrnah, I had this undeniable desire to test it. If a skill was good, how good was it? How strong was it? How do you measure exactly how strong a skill is without breaking it?

This is what happened in Week Eight when I had to focus on trimming Myrnah's hooves again. If I had been smart, I would have repeated exactly the steps I had taken successfully to trim Myrnah's hooves the first time.

I was not smart; I was ambitious.

Before I go into how I got overly ambitious during our hoof-trimming practice, this might be a good time to explain the various types of *active leadership* we can use, and their contrast: *passive leadership*.

Leadership in general is to make decisions that others will be in harmony with. When there is no harmony after the decision, there is no leadership, only a power struggle. The kinds of active leadership fall onto a spectrum:

★ Most of us are familiar with *dominance-based leadership*, where we use pressure to make horses do things they may have an instinct to fight against. Dominance-based leadership is simply a series of decisions made in a way to manage the fight-or-flight responses of a horse and ultimately get an agreement and harmony between the leader (the trainer) and the follower (the horse).

★ Note this should not be confused with *abusive leadership*, where decisions are made in such a way that lasting physical or emotional damage is created in the follower before harmony is achieved. Abusive leadership can be accidental when dominance is used to a degree that is not aware of the sensitivity of the follower. The only time abusive leadership might be potentially justifiable would be in a situation of saving a horse's life (an example might be forcing the horse into a trailer to escape fire or flood) and then accepting the consequential rehabilitation from the abuse that would need to be done afterward.

★ *Insistent leadership* is where most well-intentioned horse trainers end up on the leadership spectrum. It is not inherently better for the horse than dominance-based leadership, but it tends to be more comfortable for many humans. This is where the horse will do what you ask without much argument, but you still need your halter to do it. Or where you can ask without the halter on, but you must ask repeatedly before you get the response you seek. Insistent leadership is a series of decisions that push through a horse's resistance—below the level of fight or flight, but through resistance none the less.

★ *Assertive leadership* is what we all want. This is where you ask, and the horse says yes, settling into harmony with your choice without hesitation and without the need for any additional tools or pressure.

Most training work starts with dominance-based leadership, managing a horse's fight-or-flight instinct to get an agreement with human decisions. Halter training foals is a good example of this, when you don't allow them to run away or push into you. With practice, horses realize the halter allows them to go new places and have good experiences and so they fight against the pressure less and less, until it is possible to train insistently without needing to even pull on the rope anymore. In time, so much trust is developed in human decisions that a halter or the potential of food is no longer needed to invite the horse to go somewhere with you, and at that point, you are using assertive leadership.

I am offering another training path to develop into assertive leadership, not because I think dominance-based training is bad (I think it can be quite good), but simply because I don't enjoy it.

The kind of active leadership I start with is *supportive leadership*. This is made up of simply the personal decisions I make for my human body around horses. Horses are free to pay attention or ignore me as they choose. It is only over time, and with good timing they will start to see this kind of leadership as a motivation to seek harmony.

First, I must use supportive leadership as a consistent link to the moments horses feel "less good" for any reason. When horses feel "less good," they appreciate a little distraction from those feelings, and they start to see me as useful and helpful. Training is all about contrast, though, so there must be another kind of leadership that is even better than me being useful and helpful to the horse.

Passive leadership is for those moments when horses feel better naturally. In the moments when harmony is easy, their five senses are activated in a curious way and they want more of the way they feel without distraction. They don't need help from me, and I show them I understand that by being passive and in harmony with their movements. This is the goal—a horse can feel good without any help or dependency while gaining companionship and understanding from a herd mate (me).

Emotions run in cycles; there will always be "better" and "worse" moments. If I can be supportive once again before horses have had enough of the good feeling we may have shared passively (without distraction), they will want more of that passivity! But if I stay passive for too long, a horse will start to get concerned. This is natural and normal. The concern triggers the need to make the distance or position different between partners at some point, and it will either be the horse or the human that makes that change. If I can notice a rise in stress in the horse *before* it crosses the line to concern, I can make the change *before* the horse needs to, and I will not have been passive too long.

If I am frequently passive for too long, the horse and I will develop a worse association with passivity. The horse will gradually want more and more active support from me, and less and less passive. All simply because of timing. Having too much of something makes you want something different.

The desire for more action instead of more passivity makes training without the pressure of tools or food very difficult. When horses develop a pattern of always wanting more action, they also develop a constant desire for change and a mental pattern that nothing is ever good enough the way it is. The key to training in freedom is first for the horse to desire passivity over activity, and then for the horse to notice the pattern. What was focused on or done to get the attention and resulting passivity of the human?

Herd animals are bonded together by attention—*getting* attention or *giving* attention.

Horses can get attention by activating themselves *mentally, emotionally,* or *physically*. When they get attention by changing their thoughts or feelings, they will develop more capacity for those practices. When they get attention by taking *physical action*, they will fall into a pattern of always trying to change something, instead of being content in the current moment. When the horse uses physical action to cause passivity in the human, the horse is being the leader, making the decisions about whether to be farther apart or closer together. It isn't "bad" for the horse to be the decision maker, but if this is the habit you develop, you had better hope you like the horse's training plan for you!

When instead the horse has been encouraged to use a *focus change* to get the human's attention, causing the human to become passive and in harmony with that focus, the human has decided their position and distance from each other. If they can maintain that position, in front, behind, left side, right side, far away, close, or touching, the human maintains passive leadership.

The more horses enjoy the passive and supportive decisions humans make, the more horses will want to spend time and energy interacting with those humans. The emotional training is then in place, and the mental and physical training can begin.

Moments of passive leadership and harmony can also become extrinsic motivators to "do more of a thing," simply because of the association you can build between passivity and feeling by using timing. While you may not have caused the horse to feel good *directly*, because of the repetitions of feeling good every time you are in harmony, it starts to become a self-fulfilling prophecy (passivity in you equals "feel good" in the horse) in the horse's mind. Horses may then start to avoid active supportive leadership by looking for ways to cause us to come back into passive harmony as often as they can. It doesn't take them long to realize the flick of an ear, or the turn of the eye to notice something (curiosity and focus change), catches our attention and is rewarded with the response of passivity (harmony). The result is, we didn't make them "feel worse" by being active around them, but through timing, we built an association related with "feeling better." Supportive action is helpful and distracting, but not quite as nice as the alternative of passivity where the horse feels as good as possible internally and doesn't need or want that distraction. They only want companionship to fill their instinctual needs as a herd animal.

Now, how can this lead to what I said we all want—*assertive leadership*?

I have found that it can...but so very slowly! Probably more slowly than you are imagining!

This slow path from *supportive* and *passive leadership* to *assertive leadership* is about using simple good timing over a huge number of accurate repetitions to:

1. Link "better" feelings to passive leadership so the horse seeks supportive leadership less often.

2. Use supportive leadership to help the horse progress from solving basic needs problems, to safety problems, to companionship problems, to entertainment problems.

3. Add a cue to movements that happen naturally while in harmony, with enough repetition so they become linked. For example, fingertip pressure on the side of the withers when turning left or right, tapping on the shoulder when backing up a step, or fingertip pressure on the back of the ribs when moving the hindquarters left or right.

4. Once associations and links are made, use cues to help horses find new sources of "good feelings" they wouldn't have thought of themselves, to build more desire for entertainment—which can come in the form of training input from you.

The process really is beautiful but such a slow development that most humans will only use it in small pockets of time to augment other types of training.

I wish I had slowed down when it came to Myrnah's second hoof trim. I wish I had worked gently through supportive and passive leadership until I could achieve assertive leadership. I wish I had done things differently for Myrnah, but for me and my learning perhaps it was best that I tested the edges of what was possible, at times breaking the skills we had built. When you break something, you have an opportunity to learn all the component parts and how to put them back together again.

Insistence

A slightly less slow training option exists if you are willing to use a little insistent leadership before you get to assertive leadership.

To do this we go from *supportive leadership*, where horses are free to notice our movements around them or ignore us, to *insistent leadership*, where we start to do things that might scare or irritate them if we repeat them too many times. We touch the edge of tolerance but hopefully don't cross the line to intolerance. This motivates the horse extrinsically to change focus sooner, catch our attention, and put us back into passivity.

For example, if I stroke the horse's leg in the same place over and over, it might feel nice the first ten or twenty times, but if I keep doing the same thing the muscles are going to start tightening, and the horse is going to start stomping his foot or swishing his tail or pull away or push into me. Those would be signs the horse did not agree with me and did not find harmony, and therefore my insistent leadership had failed. If, however, I stroke that place on the horse's leg *just until I see the beginnings of muscle tightness* and then shift to a different action before crossing the line where the horse needs to defend himself, then the horse has a chance to figure out a cooperative way of communicating that he would really like me to stop touching the edge of irritation or fear.

Obviously, this is all on a spectrum—the closer you get to the edge of irritation, the bigger the motivation, and the faster the training (potentially). Whereas the more subtle you are about this insistence to change focus, the deeper the motivation will be, the more intrinsic rather than extrinsic it will be, and the slower the training (probably).

With Myrnah, approaching our second hoof trim, I wanted faster progress, and I chose to get as close to that edge as I thought I could get away with, without resorting to food rewards, ropes, or the pressure of fences. That meant withholding passivity and harmony until she tried harder to work with me at a higher level of problem-solving than she would have chosen naturally.

Hoof trimming was still new enough it was all my idea and a novelty she wasn't entirely sure she enjoyed. I decided I was going to insist she liked it, whether she liked it or not.

I am so very embarrassed to admit that was my training stance, but it was.

When I was trimming a hoof, I wanted to hold it up off the ground for as long as I wanted to, and that was longer than Myrnah was comfortable with. Inevitably, she would begin to feel trapped and try to pull her foot away gently. I would hang onto it, hoping she would regulate her emotions by thinking about something else so I could put the foot down in a "better feeling" moment, not a fight moment. It might have worked to insist this way if I had her in a halter, was feeding her a limited food resource, or her body was penned or contained in some way. Alas, Myrnah was free to walk away, and she did so repeatedly. She didn't have to go to dramatic flight or fight me hard; she was far stronger than me, and as a fully grown adult horse who had never lost a fight to a human as most domestic horses have, Myrnah didn't question her ability to walk away quietly and calmly when she felt I was being unreasonable.

Did I change my training plan? No. I was not that wise yet.

Instead, I tried the "insanity route," repeating the same action again and again, hoping for different results. Eventually, I had a horse that wouldn't even let me touch her leg without calmly walking away and ending the conversation.

Who in the world did I think I was to believe I could train a horse in total freedom? The situation was stupidly frustrating. Still, I had promised a full year of attempting to do this idiotic thing, so I decided I would bend a little and try a different type of insistence.

I lowered the intensity a little to be more reasonable. I was still going to withhold the harmony Myrnah wanted until she tried harder to work with me, but I was going to offer a less challenging type of action and two different choices of harmony and passivity for her to choose from: If she wanted to walk in a curious mental state, we could walk together in harmony, and she could show me things that were interesting to her. If she wanted to stand with me holding up one of her hooves, I wouldn't rasp the foot, we could just rest like that, in harmony. Those were our two options of passivity. If she didn't seem keen on either of those options, I would groom her while occasionally and briefly touching her legs, staying active until the very best category focus changes happened to help her feel safer and "better," and allow me to offer her brief moments of passivity to mark the feeling.

Myrnah loved being groomed, so for a while, while our training progress was insanely slow, she did get very clean and was very happy with the new plan. Checking for safety with focus changes as our priority, and walking together in the forest where she could show me all her favorite things in companionship, was priority number two. Small amounts of picking up a foot when I asked and resting standing on three legs provided the novelty of entertainment. Most importantly, I always released the foot to do something else before what I was asking became overwhelming.

I think the grooming she loved in the form of *insistent leadership* distracted me from my frustration as much as it perhaps distracted Myrnah and inspired her to check her safety a little more often. Eventually, she started to crave a little more harmony and was willing to consider once again the *assertive leadership* of me asking her to pick up her hoof and then stand on three legs as a reasonable pathway to passive harmony between us—so long as I didn't try to do any actual trimming.

Over several days, I managed to carefully rebuild what I had broken. I slowly started to rasp a little without doing it too long, and I made sure to alternate it with other types of action that were more tolerable for Myrnah. Most importantly, I paused to be passive in the moments she focused on things that I knew made her feel safe and aware.

Even insistent leadership must be reasonable enough that the horse doesn't want to get away or fight you. I had mistakenly strayed into dominant territory, without the means to manage Myrnah's desire to leave. Lesson learned. I would attempt to make wiser decisions in the future.

Or so I promised myself in that moment.

Hugs Before Riding

The debacle over hoof trimming was a lesson I would need to learn a few more times and in a few different ways. There were many skills I would need to build, break, and then build again as my understanding grew. But it was time for Myrnah and I to turn our attention toward an easier task: the skills we needed before riding.

It is strange to think that I thought this might be easier, but what I was learning was that holding one point of focus, as hoof trimming tended to require, demanded more emotional stability from a horse than activities full of distractions and varied support. Distractions and support helped in finding the next good feeling, and then the next good feeling, again and again, *together*.

I was discovering that when training in freedom, every skill needed to be broken down into much smaller components than it had in my past training life, when I had used more extrinsic motivation. The components needed for riding were fun for me to break down in this way and led to many opportunities of increased awareness for both Myrnah and me.

The first of these pieces was the "hug," to teach her to be okay being squeezed, as she might experience in different ways with a rider on her back. I was pleasantly surprised Myrnah didn't really need me to break this down. She seemed to like the sensation when I threw my arms around her neck. She shifted focus to me and "hugged me back," her neck reciprocating in an arc around my body. I released the hug while she still wanted more. From there we slowly built up to all sorts of intensities and durations. It was easy and fun.

If hugs hadn't been easy for Myrnah, I could have started with one arm, or even a fingertip crossing the centerline from her right side to left.

I could have started with the simple feeling of compression between my two hands on various places around her body, releasing and moving to a different action before I caused fight or flight. I could have alternated that reach into a hug or compression between my hands with other more acceptable actions, pausing to mark the best feelings and focus changes even if the hug or compression wasn't yet what triggered the better feelings.

Yes, the goal was to squeeze Myrnah to a better feeling, but I knew it would be okay to alternate types of squeezing with other actions that were more likely to lead to that better feeling. For a while it might be stroking her neck, followed by a brief squeeze between my hands, followed by combing her mane with my fingers—all a path of actions leading to the focus change that made her feel better and could be marked by passivity, remembered, and repeated. The squeeze itself didn't need to be the cause of the curiosity, as long as it was somewhere in the linked actions that ended with curiosity. Then, little by little, squeezing would feel better by association, until it was the only action needed to cause curiosity in Myrnah.

Once we had the basic concept of hugs causing curiosity, then it was a game of variations. How many different ways could I "squeeze her into feeling better"? How many different environments could we practice in? Could we generalize this skill until the association was so strong she couldn't imagine anything other than feeling better when she was squeezed?

This was a prerequisite for riding because sometimes riders lose balance, and I knew as a rider I was not immune to that difficulty. The potential of losing my balance while riding wasn't an "if," it was a "when," and I wanted to be sure that when I gripped with my knees, Myrnah would become curious, aware, interested, and more cooperative in response to that sensation.

Then, I had to think, what other skills did Myrnah need before being ridden?

Bounces, Backups, and Bends Before Riding

I bounced a little on the ground beside Myrnah, and she was curious. I stopped bouncing, and she wanted me to do more to trigger more curiosity in her.

If the bouncing had startled her or seemed difficult for her to accept, I could have lowered the intensity of the bounce and alternated a tiny bounce with an increased amount of time spent doing other more acceptable actions, like walking around her and pausing for moments of passivity to mark every better feeling until, almost accidentally, the tiny bounce was linked to curiosity instead of concern. Then we could have slowly built the intensity up to my bouncing as a direct cause of curiosity.

Once we had the basic association that bounces caused curiosity, I intensified them to "belly bumps," where I held onto Myrnah's withers with one hand and placed the other hand on her back, jumping up beside her to bump my belly against hers, then sliding to the ground and repeating again. At first, I expected Myrnah to be offended or startled by this activity, but she wasn't. She seemed to consider it fun, and while it made me laugh, it made her change focus and feel safer, and she seemed to wonder what novelty I might introduce next.

The key was once again in the timing, leaving her wanting more, not less, of every skill I introduced.

The reason we needed bounces and belly bumps before riding was simply because getting on and off a horse often requires jumping-type actions and contact against the horse's side. If I were to scare Myrnah while bouncing as I was getting on or off, she would not want to have me do it again. If, however, I inspired more curiosity and interest in those actions, we had a chance the riding associated with the bouncing might develop in her the same kinds of curiosity, interest, and general good feelings.

↓ Myrnah's desire to see what novel experiences I brought each day fueled our learning.

/ PART II / *Gathering Inspiration from Experience*

↓ The feel of a backup that is intrinsically motivated is different from an obedient backup. I would only learn this later.

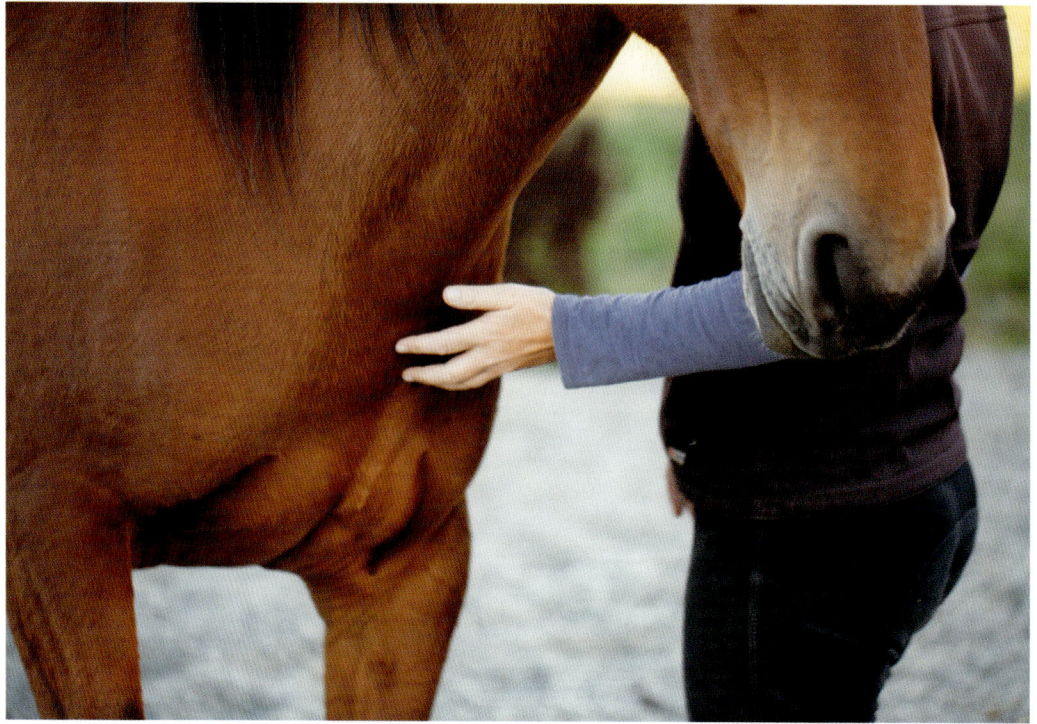

The backup was the next skill I felt needed a positive association before I considered riding Myrnah. Backing up, a form of yielding, is simply an exaggeration of slowing or stopping, and to be safe on her back, I needed to be sure we could slow or stop together whenever I asked.

Backup was an assertive leadership skill I had already practiced a lot. At that point in our training, it didn't trigger strong curiosity in Myrnah, but it was normalized and not difficult to get her to do. At the time, I thought that was enough, and it wouldn't be until later

/ * see page 71 /
/ * see page 62 /

that I would learn the link between *yields* and *feeling* was one of my training "holes" that could have been fixed with a simple shift to better timing.* During this skill-building period, we simply did a lot of backup, and I considered obedience a fun outcome for me and an acceptable outcome for Myrnah.

The neck bend was a fun and easy skill to practice as we had already spent time on it when preparing for her second round of vaccinations.* We had started with my fingertips reaching under Myrnah's jaw to wrap around the far side of her muzzle—first to stroke, then to rock, and eventually to turn the nose in my direction, always pausing when I could see Myrnah felt "better" with an engagement of her senses along with the soft physical response to my fingers.

Once this yield to fingertips was a solid habit from the far side of the muzzle, then I could move it higher up the jaw, and then over the top of the neck to the far side of the poll, then to the upper neck, then to the mid neck, then to the base of the neck, and then to the withers. Each position linked positively to the feelings of the pattern developed before it.

Because neck bends felt good to Myrnah, causing curiosity in her every time, they felt good to me too, and the more we practiced, the stronger that habitual pattern of curiosity became.

This skill would become our left and right turns when I was riding her, as well as a way to ask her to look back at me and check in when I wanted reassurance that she could shift to leader focus, remembering *I* was making decisions that would help her feel better with us in harmony.

I had come up with four components I wanted to have in place before riding—hugs, bounces, backup, and neck bends. I needed to have good associations built around each component, and each component was built from all the logical puzzle pieces you might expect, and every puzzle piece with its own good associations from past experiences. There was a fifth component I still needed to build in Myrnah, and this one would take deep study to figure out.

/ PART II / *Gathering Inspiration from Experience*

The Pre-Ride Pattern

I think it will be easiest to understand the process if we look again at the first four components I wanted confirmed in Myrnah before riding her, and then take you through my journey to find the fifth.

1. *Hugs*—This is about preparing the horse for the inevitable squeezing we involuntarily do as riders anytime we get startled. You can claim all you want that you would never grab hold of the horse with your knees or your hands, but I promise you, if you ride at speed and something startles you both, the survival instinct will kick in, and you will indeed squeeze the horse in some way. It is best if you build in the horse a habitual emotional response of curiosity and awareness to that sensation.

2. *Bounces*—To sit on a horse, you will need to get on, and you will need to get off at some point. I highly doubt every mount and dismount will go as completely gracefully as you intend. When you scare horses as you get on or off, they will not want you to get on or off again. By linking the awareness of sudden human movements up and down and bumping against their barrel to curiosity, then horses are forever entertained by your graceless moments instead of scared by them.

3. *Backup*—There will be a time while you are riding when emotions run a bit hot. When this happens, horses are likely to get defensive and act out fight-or-flight behaviors. The faster they go, the quicker they may feel overwhelmed. A backup is just an exaggerated stop, and when you have developed a strong association between curiosity and backup, you should be able to slow and stop horses at any time

/ * see page 65 /

to help them recalibrate their emotional state. The more positive the association is with backing up, the more likely you are to be able to help the horse, even if your timing is a little later than it should have been during an increasing risk of overwhelm.

4. *Neck Bends*—When horses start thinking defensively, they start solely focusing on their own needs, sometimes to the degree that they forget they are carrying a rider and are surprised or more overwhelmed when that rider makes a move to remind them this is a team sport. The neck bend can be taught on the ground as described earlier.* This is an extreme version of the skill because exaggeration makes it easier to teach. When used in the saddle, and when traveling at faster speeds, it becomes your left and right turns, allowing you to just see horses glance back out of the corner of their eye on each turn. They see you, you see them, and you are them "in this" together.

After working on these first four skills on the ground, I addressed the fifth component: the "pre-ride pattern." This is, in my opinion, the most important component of preparing a horse to ride. It means making whatever you do before you ride consistent so horses know what is coming next and can "opt in" or "out" by the way they respond to the pattern.

First, you need to build good associations with whatever the pattern is. It might be that you put one hand on the withers and one hand on the back and jump three times before vaulting on. It might be that you adjust your belt and pull up your pants. It might be that you line the horse up at the mounting block or swing one leg to loosen it before swinging it on. Whatever it is, you must first teach horses to be curious about it so they look forward to how that pattern makes them feel. *Then* you can show them that sitting on their back (for a reasonable amount of time) follows that known pattern. If they evade the known and enjoyable pre-ride pattern the next time you do it, either sitting on their back didn't feel reasonable to them, or they have another reason to avoid the experience, such as an unusual pain or exhaustion. Since horses don't have the words to explain how one day might be different from another day, an established pre-ride pattern gives them a reasonable way to show you they are up for a ride, or a reasonable way to question it.

With Myrnah, four out of the five training components went like clockwork—the hugs, the bounces, the backup, and the neck bend. Her

←↖↓ Myrnah's curiosity was infectious, and the two of us had a lot of fun playing together.

curiosity was infectious, and the two of us had a lot of fun playing together.

The pre-ride pattern was where we struggled, and we had to review all the puzzle pieces over and over to try and find what I was missing.

Training puzzle pieces are built out of physical skills, each with their own good feeling association, built from good timing and a strong foundation of feeling safe and understood during the process. It is only in hindsight I am now able to make a list of these puzzle pieces like the one that follows and see the through line of development. Understanding which tasks need positive association before the next task (puzzle piece) can be fit to it is the key.

1. *Supportive leadership* (using action around the horse until passivity is possible).

/ PART II / *Gathering Inspiration from Experience*

2. *Passive leadership* (pausing in passivity and harmony to mark moments of cooperative thinking).

3. *Rocking the horse* (moving the body or a part of the body back and forth through supportive or insistent leadership).

4. *Yielding the horse, one movement* (asking the horse to move away, one step, through assertive leadership).

5. *Assertive flow* (yielding the horse in repetitions, multiple steps, to get the *focus* we want).

6. *Drive to assertive flow* (yielding the horse in repetitions to the *action* and focus we want).

7. *Drive to short draw* (inviting the horse to follow a few steps to a target).

8. *Drive to long draw* (inviting the horse to follow a longer distance in assertive flow).

9. *Drive into draw* (moving one part of the horse's body farther from us while another part of the body comes closer to us).

Now, let me explain each of the actions that appears on the list above in more detail and how well Myrnah and I had prepared for putting them all together.

★ Our *supportive leadership* was good and Myrnah was quick to offer focus changes and increasing awareness, even when she knew she was allowed to ignore me and I wouldn't intensify the pressure.

★ Our *passive leadership* was something we both craved more of always, and it was easy to mark the cooperative thinking I thought was most beneficial to Myrnah's well-being.

★ *Rocking* to a better feeling was coming along nicely. It was perhaps a bit more insistent than it was supportive, but I was content that Myrnah was responding readily enough to change her focus when I suggested it by rocking her.

★ *Yielding one step* of movement was perhaps where things started to break down. Myrnah was obedient, but not curious as a result. I wasn't sure how to fix that at the time, so I had settled for obedience as "good enough."

- *Assertive flow*, yielding the horse in repetitions to get the focus I wanted, was a reasonable skill. It took a little insistence, but not much, and she always seemed to feel better for the exercise.

- *Drive to assertive flow* in movement was a task we could generally argue our way through. There was some resistance, but not enough to make either of us hate it, and it did always feel better once we were off and walking together. Was it a fight or was it a game? A fight is where one of you wants to leave at the end of the argument. A game is where the argument leads to you knowing each other better and wanting to stay together in harmony afterward. This skill fell in the shades of gray, my insistent leadership persisting until Myrnah was willing to move in the direction I wanted at the speed I wanted with the focus that made her feel better.... Overall it was a skill that needed improvement.

- *Drive to short draw*—Myrnah following me a short distance—was such a good skill for us. As you learned in earlier pages, we had started practicing it far too early, and we had broken it and repaired it a million times. We knew each other deeply because of each rupture and repair we had gone through. It was a hard-won skill, but we had invested so much into perfecting the timing around it, that this one was strong.

- *Drive to long draw*, however, was broken almost beyond repair. The moment I stopped holding out the finish target of my hand to touch as the end goal of the draw and walked farther away, expecting Myrnah to follow, her frustration would set in intensely with ears pinned. She *wanted* to catch me, and I was just walking away! I couldn't seem to wrap my head around the timing for her to enjoy this exercise, and I always seemed to be asking too much, too soon, leaving Myrnah repeatedly irritated, building bad association after bad association. I know now it was the foundation underneath this skill that was broken. *Drive creates draw*, or said in a better way, *good drive with positive associations creates good draw with positive associations*. That one-step yield we couldn't quite figure out and the drive to assertive flow we struggled with both needed to have better associations before I was going to succeed with the longer draw skills.

- *Drive into draw* was where it started getting fun. Technically, I would have been better off making my foundation stronger before working on this skill, but I didn't have the patience for that. Lucky for me, the strong positive associations with my short draw made up for a myriad of other flaws. I could touch Myrnah anywhere to drive her away—the hip, or the ribs, or the outside of the neck—and if my target hand was close enough to reach for easily, she was happy to oblige moving one part of her body farther away from me while she drew another part of her body closer to me. This was how I taught her to line up to the mounting block beautifully, and perhaps where I got the wrong impression that I was farther ahead in my training than I was in Myrnah's mind.

Looking at my puzzle pieces, I mistakenly decided that *drive to assertive flow* in movement was the piece I could improve to make my pre-ride pattern better.

I had been trying to get Myrnah to follow me on a long draw to the mounting block, and she seemed increasingly grumpy every time we tried it, leaving both of us with a bad taste in our mouths about this pattern. Drive into draw worked to line her up correctly next to the mounting block and would then somewhat soothe Myrnah's ruffled feathers, but the overall pattern was getting worse with repetitions, not better, telling me something needed to change.

I tackled our *drive to assertive flow* skill with a ferocious determination to make it better. I did this by practicing walking together in directions I wanted Myrnah to walk, at speeds I wanted her to walk, until we found the mounting block together, at which point we lined up for a rest. We worked so diligently that it became a normal and accepted practice with less and less resistance. But less resistance was not increased curiosity or increased good feeling.

I think a part of me knew that we were not fully ready the first couple of times I decided to sit on Myrnah's back, but I talked myself out of that doubt and went ahead with it anyway, setting us up for success through environmental factors. I chose a time of day I knew she was usually hungry, and I made sure there was fresh hay in one of the many places in the forest she might choose to take us, and there happened to be a large rock nearby to help me climb on while she was eating.

I had checked my five pre-requisites and felt four of the five were very good, and the fifth was good enough.

Eating is a form of rest. Horses get into the rhythm of chewing and that tends to lull them

↓ How strong does our harmony need to be before we test it? The only way we find out is by testing it.

into a state where they are not taking in much other information. In this case, it worked to my benefit, as Myrnah didn't seem to mind at all when I was suddenly sitting on her back. I used the same routine building up to sitting on Myrnah's back two days in a row, and then on the third day, I decided that using food as I had been was cheating the rules I had set for myself for this project. It all seemed too easy, and I wasn't sure if she had even noticed me up there on her back. It was a technicality, but I wasn't happy with it. No food had been withheld, there were many options to eat the same food in other places, and eating was a part of Myrnah's normal life. As such, I rationalized, it could be an incidental part of our training, so long as I knew Myrnah had a choice about whether to engage with it or not. However, I wanted my riding to be a voluntary activity we did together, and testing that idea when she *wasn't* eating seemed the best way to prove the theory.

Sometimes I wonder what my training project might have been like if I could have learned more of it the "easy way," through consistent small steps of development. Instead, I set myself up for failure, time and time again, attempting leaps of difficulty due to my dogged and determined impatience to do more.

– END OF PART TWO –
*Gathering Inspiration
from Experience*

Taming Wild
ELSA SINCLAIR

PART THREE

Feelings Become More Important Than Actions

PART THREE

*Feelings Become
More Important
Than Actions*

Emotions Within Actions

As soon as there was no food involved to help Myrnah rest and lower her sensory input, she did indeed find being ridden to be overwhelming and no longer offered to follow through on our pre-ride pattern. She no longer was willing to stand by the rock while I climbed on.

I was frustrated with myself for rushing this step. I had set my rules of conduct for a reason, and if Myrnah wasn't ready, she wasn't ready. My job was clearly to go back a step or more and firm up our foundation of skills.

We pulled back to reinforcing a better sense of safety through category focus changes. Remember, they are:

★ The focus on the self (looking like the ears falling out to the side and the eyes glazing over).

★ The focus on the herd (looking like checking on anyone that might communicate).

★ The focus on the environment (looking like checking on any objects without communication).

★ The focus on the leader (looking like checking on anyone who was making a current decision leading to harmony).

↓ Myrnah would often nuzzle me gently or blow on my neck in the moments I was lost in my own thoughts.

★ The focus on learning (looking like gathering extra information about any one point by using multiple senses in multiple ways).

When I took action around Myrnah, or rocked her body, or asked her to yield, the goal was for her to have to pay attention to something new, preferably in a different focus category: *self, herd, environment, leader,* or *learning*. When she noticed something new, I would become passive to allow her the best chance of remembering the information she had gathered, feeling safer with each focus change.

We alternated our practice of category focus changes with longer walks of the companionship variety where she got to show me all the things she enjoyed. We started walking out away from the home paddocks for longer excursions, more time in flow and harmony, and less time arguing about the details.

I found Myrnah's expressions of affection dramatically increased during this time. She would often nuzzle me gently or blow on my neck in the moments I was lost in my own thoughts. Through this time of accepting our limitations around riding and related skills, our relationship blossomed in new ways I hadn't expected. Instead of working on the "big picture" of what I wanted to accomplish, I set out to solidify habits of feeling, using the psychology I understood to achieve that.

Horses don't have words to communicate, they have movements instead. Movements of the eyes and the ears, the nose, and they also communicate with the bigger and more obvious movements of *yielding*. A yield can be asked for or volunteered. It is simply to move away from another, in such a way that harmony can be maintained or easily reestablished.

Yields tend to be linked to emotional states, and we can read horses' emotional stability in how comfortable or confident they are in the different yields:

★ *Backward*—Backing up is synonymous with settling into an emotional *follow position* instead of a *lead position* in a relationship. This means allowing someone else to make the decisions. When horses have trouble flowing with or being curious about decisions made by others, a solution is to develop more curiosity in backing up to strengthen that emotional confidence.

★ *Front end, left and right*—The front-end yield is connected to a horse's sense of submission or dominance. When horses have an issue with too much fight, they need to develop more curiosity associated with yielding the front end.

★ *Hind end, left and right*—The hind-end yield is connected to a horse's sense of fear. When horses have an issue with too much flight (a tendency to bolt or move abruptly), they need to develop more curiosity associated with yielding the hind end.

★ *Up and down*—The up-and-down yield movements are connected with concern about safety. Eyes see better at the correct height for the distance of the particular concern, and feet are ready to run when down on the ground. When horses have a tendency to worry and be overly concerned, they need to develop more curiosity associated with up-and-down movements of the body.

★ *Forward*—This yield can only be worked on indirectly. To the degree other types of yield have settled, forward motion will start to have more freedom, ease, and rhythm.

The emotional component of the yield was one of the many pieces of wisdom passed on to me by a horsemanship teacher a long time ago. When I have struggled with an emotional component in training, I have often come back to this theory of physical training to find my way through it.

↓ The stronger Myrnah's capacity for emotional regulation, curiosity, and confidence got, the easier everything got.

As Myrnah and I would walk together, I would notice how often she offered to back up a bit, yield the forehand, yield the hindquarters, or move her head up or down in a way I could flow and harmonize with. I would ask myself if these actions led her to more confidence or less, and if there was any way I could position myself better through action or passivity to improve her curiosity or confidence about any of these yields. For a moment in time, I was able to let go of control, let go of asking her to do better than she was ready for, and instead notice when yields, focus changes, and feelings happened naturally.

This was what training in freedom was supposed to be about: *nurturing and encouraging healthy emotional relationships by the passive way I responded to the good focuses, good feelings, or good yields when they happened naturally.* The stronger Myrnah's capacity for emotional regulation, curiosity, and confidence got, the easier everything got, even the unexpected encounters.

The woods we wandered through were predominantly shared by deer, foxes, raccoons, birds, and the occasional sea otter—all creatures interesting and no threat to Myrnah and me. This was our sanctuary of peace and harmony, where nothing was too difficult, and everything offered an ongoing novelty of sensory discoveries. The mosses covering fallen logs called out to be touched.

The charcoal of an old burned stump from a long-ago forest fire begged to be tasted. The deer grazing across a meadow were a tableau to be watched for long peaceful minutes. The raucous ravens were always worth a pause to listen. And the soft salty sea air on a windy day filled the lungs in a different way when the breeze was just right.

Some of our explorations were harder on the senses.

A neighbor playing with new guns in endless target practice, harsh sounds of explosions echoing off the hills. Another neighbor walking her dog on a leash with the abrupt contrary movements of two beings in opposition to each other. Another neighbor burning huge piles of brush that caused thick clouds of smoke, making us wonder if our forest trails were safe. We inhabited a small pocket of peace,

The awareness that focus

and attention could be turned and turned again until we both felt better was a skill that only improved when reasonable contrasts were offered.

surrounded by people who often assaulted the senses in ways nature rarely would.

You might think this was a problem for my training project, and it was, but it was also a gift. A gift of contrast that made the beautiful a million times more beautiful in appreciation of the comparison. The awareness that focus and attention could be turned and turned again until we both felt better was a skill that only improved when reasonable contrasts were offered.

Our days out walking together turned out to be a better step forward in our relationship than I might have guessed.

Was I going to keep surfing that lovely wave of positive associations evolving without pressure? Of course not! Who has that kind of time?

↓ Myrnah made it clear the contrast between one thing feeling worse and another thing feeling better was an unacceptable extreme as long as she had the freedom to walk away. How was I going to develop training without that contrast?

Contrasts in Training

I now had a pre-ride pattern issue to solve. How was I going to re-teach Myrnah, first, to enjoy the pattern, and then to again add riding to the pattern slowly and gracefully enough to not break it (this time)?

I have mentioned before that training is the awareness of contrast. There is no way around the fact that one choice you give a horse will "feel better" in contrast to another choice you give "feeling worse." Training happens when consistency occurs and the habit of one choice over the other becomes normalized.

When we have a contrast between a "bad feeling" and a "good feeling," the learning is fast because the equine body is designed to remember bad feelings to avoid future danger. When the contrast is between "good feeling" and "better feeling," training gets a little hazy and difficult for a horse to retain. It just isn't as important to the body to remember things that don't threaten it. My choice was to either push up against "bad feelings" a little closer to make training effective, or to somehow make "good feelings" more memorable. I knew how to do the former; the latter was still a mystery to me. The difficulty lay in the freedom issue. If Myrnah noticed me causing too many "bad feelings," she was going to walk away and refuse to consider my ideas, unless I resorted to using the power of a food source like the hay, which I wasn't going to do again. So, what if I made *her* idea *my* idea before she had a chance to act on it?

I wondered if I could use walking away (or preferably walking around together) as the "bad feeling" simply by doing too much of it. I wondered about really leaning into the idea of teaching her to want *less* of one thing to exaggerate wanting *more* of another thing.

The theory in general was valid. Timing, once again, was the thing that would make it fail or succeed. The timing of knowing when

Myrnah had started to have a bit too much of the walking and wanted to find a place to stand still (which would be at the mounting block, of course).

Remember: *timing* is knowing *when* to do something, *feel* is knowing *what* to do. In this plan I had the timing solidly established, but I would fail to understand the feel of what exactly to do with my active leadership.

I thought I needed to intensify the "worse" to make the "better" moments more memorable in contrast. I decided Myrnah and I would practice many turns and more speed and more pressure with a million changes of direction while we were walking together. Then, the contrast of standing at the mounting block would be so peaceful and lovely in comparison.

The plan did work…*if* you think the ends justify the means. The mounting block started to hold more and more habits of curiosity, and Myrnah was mostly willing to stay with me to work things out. However, when we were walking together, the ear pinning got worse and our arguments about which direction to walk got worse, causing me to re-think the viability of my solution.

The whole point was to have a pre-ride pattern that was consistently enjoyed, and I seemed to be making more of the pattern about struggle instead of enjoyment.

Which puzzle piece was I still missing?

Maybe it was the turns? I was using so many turns in our walking together, and they were often an argument. I thought perhaps I should slow down and figure out how to make our turns better individually and then come back to the pre-ride pattern later.

The forehand turns were obedient if I didn't ask for too many, but *obedient* and *interested* are two different things. I didn't know how to make that skill better, so I tackled hind-end yields instead, as that was a skill I had not even attempted yet. I didn't know how to teach hind-end yields in freedom, and it was clearly time I figured it out.

I had previously taught horses their hind-end yields by controlling the front end, while pushing the hind end over. In freedom, I didn't have much control over the front end of the horse, so I had avoided pushing on the back end. But Myrnah and I had a pretty good relationship now, so I thought maybe she could handle a little more "push."

I tried it, pushing and pushing and pushing with zero yield in the horse. So, I dug in with my fingers, poking harder and harder

Every time I pushed too hard, Myrnah brought me back to the drawing board. Where was the missing piece between what we could do and what we couldn't do?

in her ribs to try and get a response.

I got a response, but it wasn't the one I wanted. Myrnah swung her hip toward me and threatened to kick.

First rule, no matter what happens in horse training, is you must survive long enough to train again tomorrow, so I did the only thing possible in the situation. I ran away, circled around, and then came back to try again. She was not going to scare me!

For the next few days, I would do things that calmed Myrnah down, alternated with trying to yield her haunches. I was unsuccessful. Each day it got worse, until eventually I couldn't touch anywhere behind the shoulder without her spinning to kick at me.

It was a disaster.

We still had a solid and friendly relationship when I only touched her in front of the shoulders and asked her to do things she had good associations with. Occasionally I would stupidly try and yield her haunches over again, and she would kick at me again, and I would jump out of the way again. Then we would go back to the good parts of our relationship to settle our nerves before attempting the impossible once more. Back to the drawing board.

My goal was for Myrnah to yield her haunches away from me when I asked. If that wasn't working, what was half of that? Or half again of that? How far did I need to break it down to find the good associations?

/ PART III / *Feelings Become More Important Than Actions*

We started with my supportive leadership, moving my body around her and pausing in passive leadership to mark focus changes and curiosity. That part was still good.

Then my supportive leadership should have progressed to the touching distance, but I had broken that by doing too much and creating bad associations with touch everywhere behind Myrnah's shoulders. To repair what I had broken, I had to use *advance and retreat* techniques with better timing. I stroked her neck and shoulder, and the ease and enjoyment of being together was blissful. As I drifted my hand behind her shoulder, I could feel the muscles start to bunch and tremor under my fingers, signaling preparation for defense. Moving this slowly, it was obvious, and I felt embarrassed by how many times in the past week I had pushed past that warning and started a fight I couldn't win, giving Myrnah good reason for her defensiveness. Now that I was moving more thoughtfully, I could do better. I retreated to the neck or shoulder to reassure us both that no fight was needed. Myrnah didn't need to yell any louder to explain how she felt; I could feel it humming through my fingers when I crossed the line into too much pressure for her.

I used advance and retreat to the edge of tolerance and then back to a place that she could accept, over and over, until something caught her attention that made her feel better—a bird singing in the tree, Cleo walking past us, or a smell on the wind. Then I would pause, beginning a distant link between that better feeling (associated with the focus change) and the previous action of stroking her behind the line of the shoulder. Little by little, we changed the feeling associated with touch this way. The better feelings started happening closer and closer to the moments I was touching farther back on her body. I still had a lot of work to do, though; being okay with touch was a long way away from the willingness to yield.

This was when I discovered how important *rocking* could be in the progression of skills.

Now that Myrnah was comfortable with touch again, what if I added movement to my body while I was touching her? If I was rocking back and forth while connected to her, she would rock back and forth a little too. It wasn't a direct ask for movement; instead, it was like a tiny yield— accidental on Myrnah's part—without moving her feet. I still would need to retreat to her neck before doing too much because I didn't want to repeat the pattern of her reaching the point of kicking at me, but it was worth a try.

Sometimes it was enough for me to rock her a little and then retreat to an easier touch action

↓ When something caught Myrnah's attention that made her feel better, then I would pause, linking the feeling with the moment.

/ PART III / *Feelings Become More Important Than Actions*

Myrnah got better and better at calming me down by showing me something different she was interested in with her eyes and her ears.

before my duration of rocking crossed the line to intolerance. Other times Myrnah would show me a thing with her eyes or ears to cause me to stop rocking and become passive again. The moments of linking curiosity to the feeling of rocking were the key! Myrnah could stop me from rocking her anytime she wanted to by focusing on something new. Once she figured that out, it was far easier than kicking at me. She had control in a cooperative way instead of a defensive way, and that was better for both of us.

At this point I became obsessive about focus changes. How many focus changes could I rock her to before I crossed the line of intolerance? If one change was good, two was better; if two was good, three was better still! I was no longer doing the rocking to get to the yield, I was now doing it to see how deeply safe I could cause Myrnah to feel through those multiple points of awareness. As I became obsessive about reassuring her need for safety, Myrnah got better and better about calming me down by showing me something different she was interested in with her eyes and her ears. She even started to do it *before* I had a chance to start rocking her again, just to keep me still.

Focus changes are mentally exhausting, and at some point, aware horses just want to rest their brain. It is at this moment, when you may be intending to rock them to a focus change, that they will offer you a step of yield instead, because it becomes easier to move the body than the brain when the brain has gotten tired, and the body has not.

The first time that accidental yield happened I went passive instantly. This had been the goal, after all.

Or was it?

I was starting to see that obedience wasn't enough. For the horse to have good associations, there had to be curiosity associated with each yield. The stepping away from pressure needed to be linked to an *improvement* in feeling, not just a *lack* of feeling. This made the game more interesting. Could I rock to a focus change, but pull away from Myrnah before she pulled away from me in that step of yield? Now, ironically, I was trying to get her *not* to yield her body, only her brain.

Then deliberately, at a separate moment, could I ask for the yield at a time when I thought I could follow the obedience with some easier action, like stroking her or rocking her more gently to the focus change after the yield? Could we get both the *action* and the *feeling* linked in a positive, motivating way?

The answer was yes, but my feel and timing needed to level up to achieve that consistency. The breakthrough was exciting—it was the kind of thing I had set out to learn when I started my Mustang project.

I wanted a horse who wanted to learn with me as much as I wanted to learn with her, and I was starting to see how that might be possible.

This discovery took me to a crossroads. What was more important to me? The experiment of proving I could train a wild horse in freedom to carry a rider? Or this feeling of understanding the tiny details that made one step of yield feel like I had uncovered the deepest secrets of horse training?

Maybe It Isn't About Riding?

Deep in winter, Myrnah and I had snow to play in, and the forest seemed all new with every adventure holding glittering patterns of frost or the soft quiet of deep drifts.

Maybe I didn't care about riding Myrnah that much. Maybe we would never solve our pre-ride pattern issue. Maybe it really was okay to let that go as a fantasy of possibility. Perhaps horses were never meant to be ridden. I had a million other training ideas to follow anyway. Myrnah was my best friend, and perhaps it was time to shift the goal to easier ideas than riding her.

But if riding wasn't the goal anymore, what was? Myrnah and I walked and walked and walked, soaking up the beauty of being together out in the world, and I thought about that question.

The way Myrnah felt in my company was more important to me than what she did. I wanted to prove that to her, first and foremost. *Training the emotional system first*. When Myrnah would look at, listen to, smell, or feel something that made her more emotionally comfortable, I would respond passively to allow her to feel it without distraction and reinforce it was as important to me as it was to her. When Myrnah couldn't find something to think about that helped her feel better, I would stay actively supportive so we could figure that puzzle out together.

That was the purity of emotional training first!

Sometimes it would drift a bit into mental training, and she would make a positive focus change just to control my actions—for example, by using her ears to listen to something. She knew that in order to get more harmony, she needed to catch my attention by focusing on something else good for her.

↓ Myrnah was my best friend, and perhaps it was time to shift the goal to easier ideas than riding.

/ PART III / *Feelings Become More Important Than Actions*

↓ I no longer wondered if she was pregnant or not—
this baby was making himself known!

Moving Home

The goal had always been to bring Myrnah into the full herd of horses down in the lowland pastures and the large expanses of space on my family's farm. By March, Myrnah's foal was dancing up a storm in her belly, and I no longer wondered if she was pregnant or not—this baby was making himself known! I wanted him growing up in a proper herd with a whole group of co-parents, as was natural to horses, so it was important I introduce Myrnah to everyone sooner rather than later.

It was a beautiful sunny day when I decided to move Myrnah—and then of course the weather turned and wind whipped as it started to hail, it was March after all. Myrnah and I walked down the hill through the first empty field, looking at the big group of horses below us in the second pasture, lower in the valley. We retreated several times before she worked up the courage to continue farther to greet her new horse friends. It has always amazed me how natural advance and retreat is for horses as they slowly work up the courage to do something they are interested in.

Myrnah had met some of the horses in the herd, as I had introduced them, one by one, earlier in the year in the smaller winter paddocks around my home. This, however, was the first time I would invite her to join the entire herd of fifteen horses as a group. Taking all the time Myrnah wanted, we walked and watched from a distance until she was ready, then she entered the herd like she had known them all her life. The younger ones she was familiar with greeted her with arched necks and shared breath, and then they all got down to the business of eating—as is so important in a windy March hailstorm. The older more settled members of the group would make time for proper introductions later, when eating felt like less of a priority.

Springtime brought the big event of a new baby and not much else to report.

Due to the newness of these friendships and for my peace of mind, I chose to bring Myrnah into a separate grass paddock each night, where she could see the others but birth her foal without them being too close to her if he came unexpectedly. In the morning when there were people around to look out for the horses throughout the day, she would go out with the big herd again. Each evening, I was pleasantly surprised to find Myrnah was willing to follow me into her private paddock. (It would be another two months before Myrnah's foal was born, but he was such an active baby, we were all fooled into thinking he would come sooner!)

I don't know whether to be pleased or embarrassed about how little there was to report in the next four months with our project. The time was beautifully ticked off with the events of a foal being born, a few new horses added to the herd, riding times stretching longer (but not too long) with new speeds and small skills uneventfully added to our shared skill set. I, for the most part, held my natural impatience at bay and followed Myrnah's timeline for the continuation of her training...until the end of July, when something about the calendar date triggered the devil in me once again.

↓ I, for the most part, held my natural impatience at bay and followed Myrnah's timeline for the continuation of her training.

/ PART III / *Feelings Become More Important Than Actions*

↓ I loved this way of being with horses more than anything I had ever known before.

Too Slow!

It was unbelievable how fast a year had flown by, and now we were down to our final month of the project. Had I done enough? Was our story worth telling? Would anyone other than me be interested in a horse training evolution this slow?

I loved this way of being with horses more than anything I had ever known before, and I felt a desperation creep in to somehow show that it was valid. How could I demonstrate it had been worth the time? How do you prove a feeling?

This desperation started to creep into my sessions with a little more push and a little less patience day by day, invading the peace we had worked so hard to secure.

Our foundation held strong and Myrnah continued to be patient with my *lack* of patience, but the resistances slowly grew bigger with each thoughtless ask for too much, too soon.

If Myrnah offered a little I asked for more. When she took me as a rider out away from the herd, leaving her foal with his adoptive aunts and uncles, I wanted her to go farther, and stay away longer. When she offered trot, I wanted canter. When she offered peace, harmony, and curiosity, I wanted action and excitement.

With each proof of graceless greed on my part, Myrnah quietly got a little less generous, until one day she flat out refused. She was happy to let me ride her, I hadn't broken that yet, but anything faster than a walk was completely out of the question. And she would no longer leave the herd.

Why was she resisting now? We had so much I still wanted to do. I knew I had to break down my steps of progress again, go back, and repair the good associations that I had broken and turned bad—*but I didn't*

Myrnah loved learning new things and exploring novelties with me.

have enough time for that. Maybe if I just went back a little, it would be enough.

I wondered if we returned to focusing on companionship so she could show me where she wanted to go, and I stopped asking her to leave the herd, if that would be concession enough to "buy" faster speeds. Riding at the walk wasn't enough for me.

It was a very messy couple of weeks. I threw riding tantrums, trying to force Myrnah to practice faster speeds, and she quietly ignored all of them in the same way she serenely looked past

↓ Myrnah was near perfect emotionally. She loved life, and even better, she loved life with me.

her rambunctious colt when he was in a high mood. I couldn't scare her, I couldn't even irritate her, she simply waited me out, ignoring my chaos until I was willing to be more reasonable.

As we approached the final week of our project, I couldn't decide if I had succeeded or failed. Myrnah was near perfect emotionally. She loved life, and even better, she loved life with me. She loved learning new things and exploring novelties with me. However, she would not allow me to bully her into anything she didn't think reasonable.

/ PART III / *Feelings Become More Important Than Actions*

↓↘ Was that a failure or a success? I didn't know anymore.

Was that a failure or a success?

Not knowing what else to do and the year's timeline coming to an end, I had no choice but to accept it. I stopped pushing and started appreciating her for all she was again. Maybe I would never do anything other than ride her at the walk for the rest of our lives. Perhaps all the trotting and cantering we had practiced was a brief gift to be remembered but not repeated.

Perhaps my luck had run out and I had finally pushed Myrnah to draw a hard line between what she would and would not do for me. Perhaps this argument had pushed us past the point of recovery.

Thank Goodness for Storms

In the final week of the project, Myrnah's generosity did indeed emerge anew. Not because I asked just right, not because I fixed what I had broken, not because I emerged as a changed human worthy of forgiveness—simply because I kept showing up, trying to do a little bit better, and I was present when luck struck.

"Luck is when preparation meets opportunity," is a quote that is often attributed to the Roman philosopher Seneca.

Quite literally, luck struck in the form of an electrical storm. In the Pacific Northwest, we don't get many of those, and when they come, they are usually mild, with only brief distant flashes of lightning and quiet rumbles of thunder. There was no reason for me to opt out of riding Myrnah the day of the storm, and as it turned out, it provided exactly the kind of environmental support we needed for what I wanted.

I wasn't expecting it, I was, in fact, quite resigned to meander around at slow speeds with Myrnah for the rest of our lives if that was all she wanted to offer. Instead, the weather was just the stimulus Myrnah needed to offer a little more spring to her step in the walk. Instead of stupidly asking her for more, I reveled in the fun I was having with her and then encouraged her to rest, remember, and be peaceful sooner than she might have chosen to do so. This led to an offer of trot, which made my heartbeat faster, all our good associations from the previous months rekindled.

Little by little, we found more and more speed in short bursts of confidence and joy, until finally I thought to try a gallop. Myrnah and I had never galloped, as our canter had never seemed solid enough or confident enough to build on. On this day, it felt different, like we were both somehow new and fresh, full of possibility.

 "Luck is when preparation meets opportunity."

↓ On this day, it felt different, like we were both somehow new and fresh, full of possibility.

It wasn't the fastest gallop, but it was more than a canter,

and it was smooth, steady, confident, and exhilarating in a way I had never quite experienced before. A gift from Myrnah, and the perfect way to wrap up our experimental year of training.

Myrnah was a riddle wrapped in a mystery inside an enigma.

Happy to teach me everything she knew to the degree I would listen.

Taming Wild
ELSA SINCLAIR

The Beach

↓ Despite the ups and downs Myrnah and I had gone through, we were here, at the beach.

I had dreams of finishing my horse film WITH A SHOT OF ME *galloping Myrnah through crashing waves* ON THE BEACH AT *sunset*

I had lived through a million repetitions of that dream as it was nurtured…and then dashed upon the rocks of reality when my impatience had gotten the best of me yet again.

Something in me still thought it might be possible, despite the ups and downs Myrnah and I had gone through, and so I rented a cabin a short walk from Long Beach, Washington. At twenty-eight miles long, as the name suggests, it is the longest continuous beach in the United States. With the crashing Pacific Ocean, drifting fog, whipping wind, and endless empty sand, it was a grand finale location worth dreaming about.

But a dream this big came with endless details to sort out.

First, Myrnah and her foal Errai had to learn to wear halters for the first time in their lives. I loved my training in freedom, but I was not willing to take a horse anywhere near fast-moving vehicles without the tools to keep them safe. I had nightmare visions of a truck breakdown with a need to unload horses on the side of a highway somewhere. I absolutely was going to train a curiosity about ropes and halters before I got anywhere near that potential disaster.

Would Myrnah hold the new entrapment against me as some sort of breach of contract? It turned out, not at all.

She was fascinated by the novel experience the halter provided, and I endeavored to show her the purpose of a halter was simply another way to support more good feelings between us. With Myrnah and Errai prepared, I borrowed a large truck and trailer from a friend, loaded up five horses, and headed the seven-hour drive south to a wildly different environment.

I didn't know if Myrnah would even consider going near the beach, but we were going to go

/ The Beach

/ TAMING WILD / *Elsa Sinclair*

live by one for a little while and ask her. It would be okay if Myrnah opted out of beach life with its loud surf and buffeting winds. If it turned out she wanted to stay at the cabin behind the safety of the dunes, I braced myself to tame my wild impatience. If it was all too much, too soon for her, I would understand.

I needn't have worried.

Over the course of a year, Myrnah had showed up again and again and again as potentially the greatest horse teacher of my life. A little sun, sand, and surf wasn't going to stop her from continuing my education. Myrnah believed in play, yield, and endless curiosity as the curriculum we followed. When I became unreasonable, she wasn't above a little needed fight to set me straight.

We did find our grand finale on a beach at sunset. It wasn't galloping through crashing waves, it was true to form—more peaceful and beautiful than anything I had dreamed up.

In three hundred and sixty-five days, Myrnah showed me that, with a little practice and a lot of curiosity, training is natural, and force is optional.

APPENDIX
Freedom Based Training—Points to Ponder

Please consider the following pages a review of practical and theoretical concepts I shared in the story of my experiment with Myrnah. This content can also help you determine ways you might incorporate Freedom Based Training in your own work with animals.

Defining Freedom

- Everything is on a spectrum. This means there is either *more freedom* or *less freedom*. When you work without tools such as ropes, halters, food rewards, or small contained spaces (fences), you see varying degrees of freedom in the horse. When implementing aspects of Freedom Based Training, *you* may draw the line anywhere you like. For me, using such tools is clearly *not* working in freedom.

- In Freedom Based Training horses are free to do anything they would like unless it crosses the line of safety. If they are going to cross that line, you need to either change the environment to make the situation safer (for example, work from outside a fence) or figure out what kind of *dominance* you are willing to use to stay safe. In my work, *dominance* simply means the ability to control a horse's fight or flight. You often will need a tool, such as those listed above, to be successfully dominant.

- Training in freedom must *lean into good memories* and *distract from bad memories*. Bad memories can only be used to train effectively in a partnership where the horse cannot leave relationships associated with the bad memories. The very nature of freedom is that the horse can walk away from situations that have the potential to feel worse. This means training in freedom will need to be primarily associated with situations that have proven likely to feel better.

- Food rewards hold an equal likelihood of causing the horse to feel worse when withheld or better when delivered. While it is possible to use food with such good timing that better feelings are more likely than worse feelings, this is not equivalent to freedom because the human is using food to control better or worse feelings in the horse.

- Training in freedom is about horses regulating their own emotions. In a normal environment, we can reinforce habits of focus and feelings with our timing of actions or passivity, and that will shape how the horse behaves and feels in the future. While in freedom, horses are responsible for their own choice of focus and feeling without overt pressure to be different.

The Basics of Freedom Based Training

- Freedom Based Training is simply the shaping of horses' memories so they build habits and patterns of thinking and working *cooperatively* instead of *defensively*. When you train the brain to think cooperatively, the body follows.

- Horses are always building a *feeling association* with an event. How horses felt the last time that event happened determines how they will interact with events like it in the future. If it is a *bad feeling*, the memory is created nearly instantly. This is how living beings avoid or defend against bad things in the future. If it is a *good feeling*, it needs two components to be remembered well: the attention of a friend or herdmate and some time in rest after the feeling. When remembered, the horse will want to repeat this experience.

- We can give attention to the horse in two ways: *active* or *passive*. *Active* is distracting in nature and makes a memory weaker as you continue adding new information to the horse's brain. *Passive* is the stopping of distraction, allowing feelings to be more fully experienced and remembered.

- *Timing is training*. It isn't so much *what* you do, as *when* you do it that shapes a horse's remembered feelings. Being *more active diffuses* the intensity of a memory, and being *more passive intensifies* the power of that memory. The moment you switch from active to passive is like shining a bright light on what you want the horse to remember best.

★ Horses are showing you what they want more of by demonstrating it. If they are more active in the body, they are demonstrating *action*—a distraction from how they feel. If quieter in the body, they are demonstrating *passivity*—a lack of distraction from how they feel (peace). When you show you understand the need for distraction or peace, you are part of the solution to find better feelings together.

★ *Bad feelings* show as *fight or flight*—a lack of harmony with others, and pushing into or pulling away from synchronicity. This is the horse thinking defensively.

★ *Good feelings* result from the horse thinking cooperatively and show as any behaviors that can be matched by a partner while using the five senses: seeing, hearing, feeling, smelling, or tasting.

★ *Neutral feelings* are expressed in a *freeze* state—the horse is not currently feeling good or bad about this situation. This is a lack of feeling on a spectrum with *healthy resting* on one end and *catatonic freeze* on the other end. In freedom, *freeze* is always temporary and moves toward either cooperation or defense.

★ The more horses see that someone else understands their feelings without trying to change them, the more cooperative they become and the better they feel. This is a *natural* outcome, not a *pressured* outcome. The natural outcome of practicing cooperation becomes training when repeated to build strong memories that the horse would like to experience again.

★ *Timing shows understanding.* You will be either early or late to take action and support the horse through distraction. When you are *early*, horses feel less and less need to show you their discomfort with fight or flight. When you are *late*, horses will feel the need to be increasingly dramatic to show you how they feel.

★ Every place you stand or touch around the horse has a horse feeling associated with it. The more places you can be *passive with a good association*, the better your relationship with your horse will be. You can see that good association by observing the activation of the horse's senses while in harmony with you.

★ Mental rest cements a memory. The longer you can be passive (after the activation of the horse's senses) without changing place or distance in relation to the horse (this can be standing still or moving together), the better the horse will remember what was felt just before the rest.

A simple way to remember the basics of Freedom Based Training is like this. The horse will feel one of three things, and it is always changing:

★ **Concern** (shows in fight or flight). When horses feel *concerned*, they need a distraction. If you don't create a distraction, they will find active ways to distract themselves from how they feel.

★ **Curiosity** (shows in the use of the five senses in harmony with others). When horses feel *curiosity* in harmony with others, they are demonstrating *cooperative thinking* and should be reinforced with attention and a lack of distraction.

★ **Comfort** (shows in the lack of feeling while in harmony with others). When horses feel *comfort,* they are in the process of forming a memory of what they felt before. This can be a good memory or a bad memory.

You want to develop good timing, so remember:

★ Concern = Active

★ Curiosity = Passive

★ Comfort = Passive or Active (depending on how you feel this potential memory benefits the relationship or not)

Freedom Based Training Progression

In order to strengthen the desire to feel things together with your horse, consider the following:

★ Passivity must have a better association than action if you want to train in freedom.

★ *Timing develops association*. Horses can only want more of something they don't have enough of.

★ To build a better association with passivity we must leave horses wanting more. This means we move our feet to change place or distance before horses feel the need to do it themselves.

★ To build a worse association with activity (not a bad association, just worse because the timing is different), we must give horses too much action or distraction so that they do not want more of it.

★ We know this training is starting to develop when horses show us more opportunities to be passive. They demonstrate what they want more of.

In order to strengthen *emotional stability* in horses, consider the following:

★ The ability to *change focus* is horses' ability to *self-regulate how they feel*. If one thing feels bad, they can "switch focus" until they find something to think about that feels better. This ability to change focus requires a kind of strength that is built from exercise.

★ "Emotional exercise" needs three things: the *feeling* (use of the senses), *attention* from another herdmate, and *rest* (peace) to remember it.

★ The moment you switch from *active to passive* shines a light on what you want the horse to remember best. Horses learn they got your attention by *changing focus*.

★ By increasing difficulty, here are the steps to mark and give the horse attention for focus changes.

Remember:

/ A / *Small focus changes* (the flick of an ear or the change of an eye).

/ B / *Category changes* (self, herd, environment, leader, learning).

/ C / *Specific category changes* (drop out the responses to the categories that are easy).

/ D / *Drawing focus changes* (when you look at something, your horse should copy you).

/ E / *Maintaining one focus* (ask your horse to "hold focus" on something important and take action every time the horse tries to think about something different).

When A is coming easily to your horse, switch to only marking B. When B is coming easily, switch to only marking C and so on. If you start to see more fight or flight, you have progressed too far, too fast. Go back and build better associations with easier focus changes.

★ Remember focus changes are exercises that make horses tired. If they are not taking enough time to rest in alternation with exercise, they will get concerned and defensive. Also, if they are not changing focus enough to be aware of their safety, they will get concerned and defensive. If they are too concerned and defensive, you will need to simplify your timing and prioritize the desire to feel things together and in general.

— *Problem-Solving and the Horse's Hierarchy of Needs*

★ Relationships need problems to solve. Either you and the horse agree on problems to solve together, or you become each other's problem to solve because you think different things are important. In freedom, you must work together and agree on the correct problem first.

★ The horse has a hierarchy of needs that point out which problem needs solving first. Some degree of the foundation needs to be built before progressing to the higher-level problems. At some point, stronger foundations will need to be secured before increasing the complexity of the higher-level problems. If you attempt to focus horses on higher-level problems before they are ready, they will instinctually get defensive and show more fight or flight.

The hierarchy, most important needs listed first, is:

/ A / Basic needs (food, water, rest, and friends).

/ B / Safety (awareness of self, herd, environment, leader, and learning).

/ C / Companionship (horses showing others their interests in harmony).

/ D / Entertainment (horses taking part in someone else's interests).

In Freedom Based Training we acknowledge the basic needs as the foundation of everything (A). Then we give horses attention with good timing when they address the safety needs by changing focus between categories (B). Naturally, as enough of the safety needs are met, horses will start to take you on walks to show you the things they are interested in (C). Once they have shown you the things *they* are interested in, they become curious about *your* interests (D).

★ We use the understanding of timing to build a desire for higher-level problems. Horses can only want more of something they don't have enough of. This means we give them attention when they are practicing awareness of safety (focus changes) but encourage them to go back to basic needs often. This intrinsically builds the desire for higher problem-solving (safety). Once they offer to show us interest in companionship, we encourage them to keep coming back to check the safety through focus changes. We keep progressing through the hierarchy like this.

★ *Intrinsic motivation* (desire from within horses) develops when they can't get enough of the higher-level problem and so want more of it. When we keep encouraging them to build their foundation better, they have the capacity to take on higher-level problems. Through this pattern, the horse guides the timeline for progression, and training naturally will reach a point where the horse desires to learn things the human finds entertaining.

Types of Leadership (Decision-Making)

★ *Passive leadership* (deciding how much space is between horse and human and what position is held).

★ *Supportive leadership* (moving around horses as a distraction to help them change focus while allowing them to make their own choices).

★ *Assertive leadership* (causing the horse to *yield* or *draw* without resistance).

★ *Insistent leadership* (causing the horse to yield, draw, or change focus through freeze-type resistance).

★ *Dominant leadership* (managing fight or flight behavior while causing the horse to yield, draw, or change focus).

★ *Abusive leadership* (pressure that causes damage while telling the horse to yield, draw, or change focus).

Freedom Based Training is naturally restricted to the first four types of leadership. Occasional dominance might be used, but if used too frequently without the tools to support it, the horse will generally choose to leave the conversation until a different kind of leadership is adopted. Abusive leadership is hopefully never used, with perhaps the exception of saving a horse's life. The human must accept the consequential rehabilitation that will need to be done afterward.

Leadership That Builds Emotional Skills

A leader is only a leader when someone agrees with him. What follows are the various ways we might make decisions around horses to find agreement and harmony.

Active leadership (distracting horses from their feelings) can take on many forms. In Freedom Based Training, we progress from the easiest type of active leadership to the most challenging type as skills grow:

/ A / *Supportive leadership* (action around horses that they are free to notice or ignore).

/ B / *Insistent leadership* (action around horses that they must respond to).

/ C / *Assertive leadership* (actions we ask horses to take with their body that they can easily say "yes" to).

The first type of active leadership we practice is *supportive*, walking around the space or stroking the horse until we see the feet quiet and the brain active (A). Then we "mark" that moment with the beginning of passive leadership to help the horse remember the feeling associated with cooperative thinking.

The second type of active leadership we practice is *insistent*. This is where we push the edge of comfort for horses by stroking them, rocking them, or being more active around them until they change focus to cause us to become passive again (B). (This insistent type of leadership is not a requirement to progress, but it does get you to the assertive type of active leadership faster.)

The third type of active leadership we practice is *assertive*. This is where we increase the pressure until horses yield the body away from it and use their senses as well (C).

We may need to alternate the different types of active leadership to get the desired result of *feeling better together*. If we cause fear or irritation in the horse, we have done too much of something, and that is a failure in judgment that we keep moving past until we find an action that is more successful (causing curiosity instead). With every failure, we learn a little more about our horse and can do better next time. *Success* is the action that results in harmony, including the use of the senses. The proper rest in passive leadership following success is the way to cement the good memories and make them repeatable.

Leadership That Builds Physical Skills

Each one of these following steps builds on the foundation of good associations with easier physical skills that have been established into habit:

- *Supportive leadership* (action around the horse until passive is possible).

- *Passive leadership* (marking moments of cooperative thinking).

- *Rocking the horse* (supportive or insistent leadership).

- *Yielding the horse, one movement* (assertive leadership).

- *Assertive flow* (yielding the horse in repetitions to maintain the focus we want).

- *Drive to assertive flow* (yielding the horse in repetitions into the action we want).

- *Drive to short draw* (horse following a few steps to a target).

- *Drive to long draw* (horse following a longer distance in assertive flow).

- *Drive into draw* (moving one part of the horse's body farther away while another part of the body comes closer).

The Emotional Components of Physical Yields

A *yield* can be asked for or volunteered. It is simply to move away from another, in such a way that both participants can stay in harmony. Yields tend to be linked to emotional states, and we can read a horse's emotional stability in how comfortable or confident he is in the different yields.

- **Backward**—Backing up is synonymous with settling into an *emotional follow position* instead of a lead position in a relationship. Allowing someone else to make the decisions. If the horse has trouble flowing with or being curious about decisions made by others, a solution is to develop more curiosity in backing up to strengthen that emotional confidence.

- **Front end, left and right**—The front-end yield is connected to a horse's *sense of submission or dominance*. If horses have an issue with too much fight, they need to develop more curiosity associated with yielding the front end.

- **Hind end, left and right**—The hind-end yield is connected to a horse's *sense of fear*. If your horse has an issue with too much flight (a tendency to bolt or move abruptly), he needs to develop more curiosity associated with yielding the hind end.

- **Up and down**—The up and down movements are connected with *concern about safety*. Eyes see better at the correct height for the distance of the particular concern, and feet are ready to run when down on the ground. If your horse has a tendency to worry and be overly concerned, he needs to develop more curiosity associated with up and down movements of the body.

- **Forward**—This yield can only be worked on *indirectly*. To the degree other emotional issues have settled, forward motion will start to have more freedom, ease, rhythm, and confidence.

Final Thoughts When Training in Freedom

- When training in freedom, emotional training must remain primarily important, mental training the secondary importance, with physical training holding the final level of importance.

- Training the *emotional system* is the development of focus changes to regulate stress levels and is learned through co-regulation and interactions with others.

- Training the *mental system* is the development of puzzle-solving. "I must do this before I get that."

- Training the *physical system* is the development of muscle strength, flexibility, and adaptability through repeated movements.

- When horses have developed emotional fitness, they can continually regulate their stress in a way that allows *cooperative thinking* instead of *defensive thinking*.

- When physical training or mental training is valued more than emotional training, horses may need the pressure of a halter, bridle, or food reward to help them regulate their stress levels enough to think cooperatively instead of defensively.

The goal of all horse training is ultimately to have more harmony between horse and rider in a variety of situations. This is a beautiful thing and perhaps the means justify the ends?

I will let you decide that for yourselves.

INDEX

/ A /

- Abusive leadership, 98–99, 185
- Action
  - in core theory, 34, 52, 55, 155
  - in emotional training, 76, 182, 183
  - vs. feelings, 75
- Active leadership, 98–101, 155
- Advance and retreat, 138, 157
- Aggression, 11, 89
- Alexander Technique, 16
- Assertive flow, 118, 119, 120, 186
- Assertive leadership, 99, 102, 185
- Attention. *See also* Focus
  - active vs. passive, 182
  - filming as, 40
  - getting vs. giving of, 87
  - in herd dynamics, 34, 68, 100–101
  - Myrnah's capacity for, 45
- Awareness
  - choice and, 58–59
  - SHELL categories of, 76–77
  - stress and, 59
  - in training, 132–33, 154

/ B /

- Backup
  - as prerequisite for riding, 110, 114
  - as yielding, 129, 185
- Beach, riding on, 175–79
- Beech tree, 3–5
- BLM. *See* Bureau of Land Management
- Body, of horse. *See* Physical system, training of
- Bounces, as prerequisite for riding, 108, 114
- Breathing, in harmony, 69
- Bucking, Demi's history of, 9–11
- Bureau of Land Management, horse adoption policies, 31, 42, 62

/ C /

- Cameras and filming
  - effects of, 77–78
  - Myrnah's awareness of, 45
  - as tool in training, 76, 146
- Centered Riding principles, 16–17
- Chewing, rhythm of, 120, 122
- Choice
  - horse's awareness of, 23–24, 58–59
  - as motivation, 95–96
  - in training, 38–39, 135
- Cleo, 50, 85
- Coercion, 48
- Comfort, as feeling state, 61, 183
- Comfort zones, 38–39
- Communication
  - movements as, 129
  - in training, 146–47

INDEX

- Companionship
  - in hierarchy of needs, 86, 89, 184
  - training with, 94, 101, 127–28, 148, 185–86
- Compression, sensation of, 106–7
- Concern, as feeling state, 61, 183
- Confidence, 129, 132, 148
- Control
  - lack of, 62
  - as training goal, 10, 37
- Conversation, training as, 146–47
- Cooperation
  - vs. defensive behavior, 68
  - in emotional fitness, 61
  - in training, 79, 96, 182, 183, 185
- Core theory, for Freedom Based Training, 31, 34, 37–39
- Curiosity, of horse
  - in emotional training, 61, 69, 76, 132–33
  - as feeling state, 183
  - in focus categories, 76–77
  - vs. relaxation, 72–73
  - in rhythm with comfort, 92–93, 151
  - timing considerations, 73–74
  - trainer awareness of, 51
  - as training feedback, 58–59, 69

/ D /

- Deadlines, pitfalls of, 37, 147
- Decision-making, leadership as, 185–86
- Defensive behaviors
  - avoiding, 66, 84, 185
  - caused by training, 88–89, 138, 182
  - vs. cooperation, 68
  - effects of, 79
- Demi, author's fights with, 9–11, 15
- Desires, of handler, 39.
  - *See also* Motivation
- Deworming, 62
- Distractions
  - in emotional training, 182
  - in "feeling better," 100–101, 106
  - hander as, 34, 142
  - horse's need for, 61
  - memory formation and, 65–66
- Dominance/domination
  - as mindset, 3–5
  - in training, 37, 72–73, 98, 182, 185

  - yielding and, 129
- Dominant leadership, 98, 182, 185
- Draglines, 47–48
- Draw skills, 118–20, 185
- Dressage lessons, rides to, 10–11
- Drive skills, 118–20, 185–86

/ E /

- Eating, as rest, 120, 122. *See also* Food
- Electrical storm anecdote, 166
- Emotional exercise, 184
- Emotional fitness, 61, 185
- Emotional stability, 61, 106, 184
- Emotional systems
  - in cooperative work, 79
  - handler awareness of, 76
  - horse's regulation of, 182
  - memory and, 65
  - motivation and, 65–66
  - regulation of, 66
  - in yielding, 129, 132, 185
- Emotional training.
  See also Freedom Based Training
  - core theory for, 31, 34, 37–39, 142
  - horse's feelings in, 58–59
  - primary importance of, 185
- Enclosures, 31, 49
- Entertainment
  - in hierarchy of needs, 86, 95, 102, 184
  - training components for, 114
- Environment-focus, 76–77
- Errai, 157–58, 176
- Excitement, in emotional fitness, 61
- Expectations
  - deadlines and, 37, 147
  - in goal-setting, 142, 146
- Experience, sharing of, 61
- Eye contact, 48–50

/ F /

- Fear, in horses, 24, 185
- Feel, of handler
  - adapted to the horse, 50
  - author's sense of, 47
  - vs. timing, 71–79, 136
- Feeling states, of horse
  - action and, 75, 147
  - building associations in, 182–84
  - contrast in, 72, 135–41, 155

  - relaxation and, 72
  - self-regulation of, 184
  - timing considerations, 154
  - training with, 58–59, 66–69, 118, 148, 182
  - yielding and, 141
- Feldenkrais Method, 16
- Fight/flight responses
  - in communication, 129
  - control of, in training, 182
  - in Mustang behavior, 44–45
  - yielding and, 185
- Fighting.
  See also Dominance/domination
  - as approach to the world, 4
  - defined, 119
  - with horses, 9–11, 15, 19–20
- Filming. *See* Cameras and filming
- Focus
  - categories of, 66–69, 76, 79, 82–84
  - holding of, 106
- Focus changes
  - in establishing leadership, 100–101
  - handler awareness of, 59, 61
  - in regulating feelings, 184
  - training with, 66–69, 92, 127–28, 140–41
- Follow position, 129
- Following, of handler, 58–59, 88–89, 92–96
- Food
  - as basic need, 24, 85, 86, 184
  - as reward, 23, 96, 182
- Force.
  See also Dominance/domination
  - avoiding, 15
  - withholding harmony as, 57
- Forest
  - as place of freedom, 9, 132–33
  - walks in, 92–96
- Forward movements, as yielding, 129, 185
- Freedom
  - author's desire for, 9–11, 16, 24
  - of choice, 23–24
  - vs. coercion, 48
  - ideal of, 42–43
  - spectrum of, 182
- Freedom Based Training.
  See also Emotional training
  - asking too much in, 57–59, 161–65

INDEX

awareness in, 58–59
breaking down components of, 106, 117–19
conception of, 24–25
contrasts of feeling in, 72, 135–41, 155
as conversation, 146–47
core theory for, 31, 34, 37–39, 185
filming of, 40, *41*
hierarchy of needs in, 95
horse's emotions in, 58–59, 61, 132–33, 135
passivity and action in, 52, 183–84
practical learning for, 37–39
progression of, 183–84
puzzle pieces of, 117–19
stress regulation in, 59
- Freeze states, 183
- Friends, as basic need, 86, 184
- Front end, yielding of, 129, 185

/ G /

- Gallop, 166–70
- Games, 119
- Goals, 142, 146

/ H /

- Habits
  cooperation as, 96
  in emotional fitness, 61
  in emotional training, 59, 68, 128, 135
  of trainer/handler, 57
- Halters, 47–48, 176
- Harmony. *See also* Passive harmony
  author's desire for, 12, 25–26, 55
  focus and, 61
  horse's desire for, 57–58, 71–72, 86
  in leadership, 98–102
  as reward, 57, 72, 101
  yielding in, 129
- Herd dynamics
  attention in, 100–101
  in gathered Mustangs, 44–45
  Myrnah and, 157
  social skills in, 34, 47, 68
- Herd-focus, 76–77
- Hierarchy of needs, 85–89, 184–85
- Hind end, yielding of, 129, 137–38, 185
- Hoof care, 81–84, 103–5

- Hugs, as prerequisite for riding, 106, 114

/ I /

- Insistent leadership, 73, 99, 103–5, 185

/ J /

- John (friend), 24–25, 47

/ K /

- Kathleen (client), 20, 22–24
- Kicking, 10, 137–38, 140

/ L /

- Lead positions, 129
- Lead ropes
  on Mustangs, 47–48
  as tool of reinforcement, 47–48, 73, 75
- Leader-focus, 76–77
- Leadership
  abusive, 98–99, 185
  active, 98–101, 155
  assertive, 99, 102, 185
  categories discussed, 98–102, 185
  dominant, 98, 185
  insistent, 73, 99, 103–5, 185
  passive, 100, 118, 155, 185–86
  Ransom's modeling of, 47
  supportive, 99–100, 102, 103, 117–18, 138, 185–86
- Learning, by handler, 10, 102, 105–6, 122
- Learning, by horse. *See also* Memory
  attention and focus in, 49, 68, 82, 106
  curiosity in, 72–73, 78
  emotional aspects, 51, 61, 135
  as focus category, 76, 77, 128
  motivation for, 95–96, 141
- Liberty horsemanship, 23
- Limits, in training, 92, 95
- Long Beach, WA, 175–79
- Luck, 166

/ M /

- Margaret (friend), 40, 42, 47, 146

- Memory
  resting states and, 51, 59, 61, 72, 78–79, 182
  shared experiences in, 65
- Mental training, 58, 59, 79, 185
- Motivation
  emotional, 65–66
  intrinsic vs. extrinsic, 95–96, 101, 103, 185
  leadership options and, 98–102
  novelty in, 95
  in training, 71, 78, 92, 95–96
- Movement
  as communication, 129
  in pre-ride pattern, 108, 110
  yielding as, 141
- Mustangs. *See also* Myrnah
  BLM adoption policies, 31, 42, 62
  Saavedra, 37–39, 47, 48–49
- Myrnah
  author's first impressions of, 45
  lessons from, 5
  pregnancy, 157
  training goals with, 50–55

/ N /

- *Naked Liberty* (Resnick), 23
- Neck bends, as prerequisite for riding, 108, 111, 115
- Neck ropes, riding with, 16
- Needs, hierarchy of, 85–89, 184–85
- Negative reinforcement, 12, 15

/ P /

- Passive harmony
  in core theory, 34, 52, 55, 155
  in emotional training, 76, 89, 103–5
  in herd dynamics, 61, 68–69
  as positive reinforcement, 52, 65–66, 78–79, 183–85
  timing of, 55, 71–74
- Passive leadership, 100, 118, 155, 185–86
- Patience
  author's lack of, 16, 25, 37, 52, 85
  importance of, 147, 148
  Myrnah's, 161
- Peace, horse's desire for, 9. *See also* Harmony

INDEX

- Pedestal, work with, 146–47
- Pens, 31, 49
- Physical system, training of, 58, 59, 79, 185–86
- Positive reinforcement
  in emotional training, 59, 65–66, 183–85
  vs. negative reinforcement, 12
  passive harmony as, 78–79
- Pre-ride patterns
  contrast of feeling in, 135–41, 148, 154
  movements of, 108, 110–11
  sequence of, 114–22
- Pressure, physical, 49, 106–7
- Pressure-based training
  eye contact in, 48–50
  levels in, 37
  limits of, 75, 96
  relaxation in, 72
  rewards in, 96
  timing and, 73–74
  uses of, 185
- Problem-solving, hierarchy of needs in, 184–85
- Puzzle pieces, of training, 117–19

/ R /

- Ransom, lessons from, 34, 47, 68
- Reinforcement
  progression on, 65–66, 68–69
  through passive harmony, 78–79
- Relaxation, 72–73
- Repetition
  in developing assertive leadership, 102, 119
  of feeling good, 101
  of physical actions, 59, 71
  pitfalls of, 58, 71, 73
- Resistance, 11, 99, 119, 120, 161–62
- Resnick Method Liberty Horsemanship, 23
- Resting states.
  See also Passive harmony
  vs. awareness, 59
  as basic need, 86, 184
  vs. catatonic freeze, 183
  duration of, 84
  eating as, 120, 122
  effects of, 79

horse's sense of safety and, 82
mental processing in, 51, 59, 61, 72, 78–79, 182–83
in training, 155
- Rewards
  food as, 23, 96, 182
  harmony as, 57, 72, 101
- Riding
  as goal, 142, 146, 147
  horse's voluntary participation in, 122, 127, 155
  preparation for, 106–11, 115–22, 154–55 (See also Pre-ride patterns)
- Rocking the horse, 118, 138, 186
- Ropes, curiosity about, 176. See also Lead ropes; Neck ropes, riding with
- Rushing. See Patience

/ S /

- Saavedra, 37–39, 47, 48–50
- Safety, horse's sense of, 79, 82–85, 87, 184–85
- Self-focus, 76–77
- Seneca, 166
- Senses, of horse
  memory and, 65
  training considerations, 51, 58–59, 183
- Shameeka, 16
- SHELL of awareness, 76–77
- Sinclair, Elsa
  blog project, 31
  early work with horses, 9–11, 16–26
  family relationships, 10–11, 12, 17, 47
- Sleeping states, 82
- Slowing down, 37, 110, 147, 148, 161
- Social skills, 34, 47, 68
- Squeezing. See Hugs
- Stops and stopping, 110, 114–15
- Stress regulation
  in focus-change goals, 66, 68–69
  senses in, 59
- Submission, 9, 48, 129
- Supportive leadership
  described, 99–100, 185–86
  training with, 102–3, 117–18, 138

/ T /

- Tellington TTouch/Equine

Awareness Method, 16
- Thriving, 4–5
- Timing
  adapted to the horse, 50
  curiosity and, 73, 75–79
  vs. feel, 71–79
  of passivity, 55, 71–74
  resting states and, 84
  in social dynamics, 47
  as training, 81, 102, 135–36, 154, 182–84
- Training. See also Emotional training; Freedom Based Training; Pressure-based training
  areas/space required for, 49
  author's blog about, 31
  limits of traditional methods of, 10, 20, 22–24, 37
  mental, 58, 59, 79, 185
  motivation and, 92
  physical, 58, 59, 79, 185–86
  relaxation in, 72
- Treats, as rewards, 23, 96, 182
- Trust, 51, 62, 65, 99

/ U /

- Up and down yield movements, 129, 185

/ V /

- Vaccinations, 62, 65, 69

/ W /

- Waking states, 82
- Walking, with horse, 92–96
- Water, in hierarchy of needs, 86, 184

/ Y /

- Yahzi, 49–50
- Yawning, Myrnah's faking of, 72, 73
- Yielding
  backing up as, 110
  as communication, 129
  emotional aspects, 141, 186
  as training puzzle piece, 118